EDITOR: Maryanne Blacker

FOOD EDITOR: Pamela Clark

■ ■ ■

ART DIRECTOR: Sue de Guingand

ARTIST: Annemarlene Hissink

■ ■ ■

ASSISTANT FOOD EDITORS: Kathy McGarry,
Louise Patniotis

ASSOCIATE FOOD EDITOR: Enid Morrison

SENIOR HOME ECONOMIST: Lovoni Welch

HOME ECONOMISTS: Janene Brooks, Emma Braz,
Justin Kerr, Nadia Kretchmer, Maria Sampsonis,
Jodie Tilse, Amal Webster

EDITORIAL COORDINATOR: Elizabeth Hooper

KITCHEN ASSISTANT: Amy Wong

■ ■ ■

STYLISTS: Marie-Helene Clauzon, Carolyn Fienberg,
Jane Hann, Cherise Koch, Sophia Young

PHOTOGRAPHERS: Robert Clark, Robert Taylor

■ ■ ■

HOME LIBRARY STAFF:

ASSISTANT EDITORS:
Mary-Anne Danaher, Lynne Testoni

EDITORIAL COORDINATOR: Lee Stephenson

■ ■ ■

CIRCULATION & MARKETING DIRECTOR:
Chris Gibson

PUBLISHER/MANAGING DIRECTOR: Colin Morrison

CHIEF EXECUTIVE OFFICER: Richard Walsh

■ ■ ■

Produced by The Australian Women's Weekly Home Library.
Cover separations by ACP Colour Graphics Pty Ltd., Sydney.
Colour separations by Network Graphics Pty. Ltd., Sydney.
Printing by Hannanprint, Sydney.
Published by ACP Publishing Pty. Limited,
54 Park Street, Sydney.
◆ AUSTRALIA: Distributed by Network Distribution
Company, 54 Park Street Sydney, (02) 282 8777.
◆ UNITED KINGDOM: Distributed in the U.K. by Australian
Consolidated Press (UK) Ltd, 20 Galowhill Rd, Brackmills,
Northampton NN4 7EE (01604) 760 456.
◆ CANADA: Distributed in Canada by Whitecap Books Ltd,
351 Lynn Ave, North Vancouver B.C. V7J 2C4 (604) 980 9852.
◆ NEW ZEALAND: Distributed in New Zealand by Netlink
Distribution Company, 17B Hargreaves St, Level 5,
College Hill, Auckland 1 (9) 302 7616.
◆ SOUTH AFRICA: Distributed in South Africa by Intermag,
PO Box 57394, Springfield 2137, Johannesburg (011) 491 7534.

■ ■ ■

Tomato Cookbook

Includes index.
ISBN 1 86396 052 X

1. Cookery (Tomatoes). Title: Australian
Women's Weekly. (Series: Australian
Women's Weekly Home Library).

641.65642

■ ■ ■

ᵃ A C P Publishing Pty. Limited 1996
ACN 053 273 546
◆ This publication is copyright. No part of it may be
reproduced or transmitted in any form without the
written permission of the publishers.

■ ■ ■

FRONT COVER: Clockwise from left: Blue Cheese
and Roasted Tomato Tart, page 75; Mixed Leaf and
Tomato Salad with Toasted Nuts, page 102;
Nutty Fettuccine Salad, page 57.
Glass bowl from H.A.G. Imports.
BACK COVER: Bottled Antipasto, page 27.

■ ■ ■

TOMATO
COOKBOOK

The humble tomato is ripe for a change of image and takes centre stage in these fabulous recipes. The natural sweetness and freshness of tomatoes adds distinctive flavour to soups, snacks, starters, lunches and main courses as well as beautiful baking and refreshing drinks. A special preserves section boasts a terrific range of oils, dressings, sauces, marinades, relishes, jams and much more, and our extensive glossary contains many helpful preserving tips.

Pamela Clark

FOOD EDITOR

D0543114

BRITISH & NORTH AMERICAN READERS: Please note that
Australian cup and spoon measurements are metric. A quick conversion
guide appears on page 127.
A glossary explaining unfamiliar terms and ingredients appears on page 120.

Preserves Plus

We've given miniumum storage times for these recipes but so much depends on factors outside our control, such as sterilisation methods, etc. (see tips on page 124). A few recipes are suitable to freeze and are marked thus **F**; however, do not freeze goods in bottles but transfer to clean plastic containers, leaving 2cm space at top for contents to expand, seal plastic containers with clean lids.

TOMATO CITRUS VINAIGRETTE

11 medium (2kg) tomatoes, chopped
2 cups (500ml) water
1/2 cup (125ml) olive oil
1 clove garlic, peeled
20cm strip orange rind
1 tablespoon drained capers
2 teaspoons yellow mustard seeds, toasted
1 teaspoon sugar
1 teaspoon salt

Combine tomatoes and water in large pan, simmer, covered, about 1 hour or until tomatoes are very soft. Strain tomato mixture through fine cloth into bowl. Allow liquid to drip through cloth slowly, do not squeeze cloth; this could take at least 3 hours. Discard pulp.

Return liquid to large pan, bring to boil, remove from heat, stir in remaining ingredients. Pour hot liquid into hot sterilised jars or bottles; seal immediately.

Makes about 1.25 litres (5 cups).
■ Storage: Refrigerated for about 2 weeks.

FRESH HERB, CHEESE AND TOMATO DRESSING

A flavour boost for salads.

1 cup (250ml) peanut oil
1/2 cup (125ml) macadamia nut oil
1/2 cup (125ml) white wine vinegar
1/3 cup (80ml) lemon juice
2 tablespoons tomato paste
1 large (250g) tomato, seeded, finely chopped
1 small (100g) red Spanish onion, finely chopped
125g blue vein cheese, chopped
1 tablespoon shredded fresh mint leaves
1 tablespoon chopped fresh coriander leaves
1 tablespoon chopped fresh parsley

Whisk oils, vinegar, juice and paste in medium bowl until combined. Stir in remaining ingredients, pour into cold sterilised jars; seal immediately.

Makes about 1 litre (4 cups).
■ Storage: Refrigerated for about 2 weeks.

HOT SUN-DRIED TOMATO MUSTARD

1/2 cup (95g) yellow mustard seeds
1/4 cup (45g) black mustard seeds
1 cup (150g) drained sun-dried tomatoes in oil
1/4 cup (60ml) olive oil
2 tablespoons balsamic vinegar
2 teaspoons salt
1 teaspoon sugar
1 1/2 tablespoons chopped fresh oregano leaves
1 teaspoon chopped fresh thyme

Combine seeds in medium bowl, cover with warm water, cover bowl; stand overnight.

Rinse seeds; drain well. Blend or process seeds, tomatoes and oil until combined. Add vinegar, salt and sugar, blend until thick. Stir in herbs. Spoon mustard into cold sterilised jars, seal immediately.

Makes about 500ml (2 cups).
■ Storage: Refrigerated for about 2 months.

From left: Hot Sun-Dried Tomato Mustard; Tomato Citrus Vinaigrette; Fresh Herb, Cheese and Tomato Dressing.

▣ TOMATO PESTO

Can be served as a dip or tossed through pasta.

**2 small (260g) tomatoes,
    peeled, chopped
1 cup (150g) drained sun-dried
    tomatoes in oil
3 cloves garlic, roughly chopped
¼ cup (40g) pine nuts, toasted
¼ cup (20g) grated romano cheese
2 tablespoons shredded
    fresh basil leaves
1 teaspoon salt
½ teaspoon cracked black
    peppercorns
½ cup (125ml) olive oil**

Blend or process both tomatoes and garlic until combined.

Add nuts, cheese, basil, salt and pepper; blend until smooth. Gradually pour in oil while motor is operating, blend until thick. Spoon pesto into cold sterilised jars, pour in a little extra oil to cover pesto completely; seal immediately.

Makes about 500ml (2 cups).

▧ Storage: Refrigerated for about 2 weeks.

▣ ROASTED TOMATO STOCK

A good base for soups and sauces.

**20 medium (1.5kg) egg tomatoes
1 teaspoon salt
1 teaspoon cracked black
    peppercorns
2 tablespoons olive oil
1 medium (350g) leek, chopped
2 medium (240g) carrots, chopped
1 large (200g) onion, chopped
250g button mushrooms, chopped
4 cloves garlic, chopped
1 cup (250ml) dry white wine
¼ cup (60ml) tomato paste
3 bay leaves
1 sprig fresh parsley
1 sprig fresh thyme
1.5 litres (6 cups) water**

Cut tomatoes in half lengthways. Combine tomatoes, salt, pepper and half the oil in large baking dish. Bake, uncovered, in moderate oven about 45 minutes or until tomatoes are very soft.

Heat remaining oil in large pan, add leek, carrots, onion, mushrooms and garlic, cook, stirring, until onion is soft. Stir in wine, paste, herbs and water, simmer, uncovered, about 35 minutes or until vegetables are soft. Add tomato mixture to pan, simmer, uncovered, 5 minutes. Press mixture through fine sieve, discard pulp. Pour hot stock into hot sterilised jars; seal immediately.

Makes about 1.5 litres (6 cups).

▧ Storage: Refrigerated for about 1 week.

TRADITIONAL TOMATO PASTE

**20 large (5kg) tomatoes, quartered
¼ cup (55g) fine sea salt
¼ cup (60ml) olive oil,
    approximately**

Place tomatoes in large bowl, sprinkle with salt; cover, stand overnight.

Rinse tomatoes; drain, press firmly through coarse sieve; discard pulp. Press puree through fine sieve; discard any seeds. Place puree in large pan, simmer, uncovered, stirring occasionally, about 3½ hours or until very thick and dark in colour. Spoon hot paste into hot sterilised jars, pour in a little olive oil to cover paste completely; seal immediately.

Makes about 750ml (3 cups).

▧ Storage: Refrigerated for about 1 year.

RHUBARB AND TOMATO CHUTNEY

1 tablespoon olive oil
1½ tablespoons black
mustard seeds
1½ tablespoons ground cumin
½ teaspoon ground cloves
1½ tablespoons ground coriander
11 medium (2kg) tomatoes,
chopped
2 large (400g) onions, chopped
1 teaspoon salt
2 cloves garlic, crushed
2 cups (340g) raisins
1 cup (200g) firmly packed
brown sugar
1 cup (250ml) brown vinegar
1 bunch (700g) 4 cups chopped
fresh rhubarb stems

Heat oil in large pan, add seeds and spices, cook, stirring, until fragrant. Add tomatoes, onions, salt, garlic, raisins, sugar and vinegar. Stir over heat, without boiling, until sugar is dissolved. Simmer, uncovered, stirring occasionally, about 35 minutes or until mixture is thick. Stir in rhubarb, simmer, uncovered, stirring occasionally, about 5 minutes or until rhubarb is tender. Spoon hot chutney into hot sterilised jars; seal immediately.

Makes about 2 litres (8 cups).

■ Storage: In cool, dark place for about 1 year; refrigerate after opening.

FIG, TOMATO AND CARAMELISED ONION JAM

The perfect complement to steak, sausages, or bacon and eggs.

1 tablespoon olive oil
4 medium (600g) onions,
thinly sliced
2 tablespoons white wine vinegar
¼ cup (55g) sugar
6 large (1.5kg) tomatoes,
peeled, chopped
3½ cups (500g) dried figs, sliced
½ cup (125ml) lemon juice
4 cups (880g) sugar, extra

Heat oil in large pan, add onions, cook, stirring, over low heat about 15 minutes or until onions are very soft. Add vinegar and sugar, cook, stirring often, over low heat about 20 minutes or until mixture is lightly browned.

Combine tomatoes with figs in large heavy-based pan. Simmer, uncovered, about 20 minutes or until fruit is pulpy. Add onion mixture with remaining ingredients, stir over heat, without boiling, until extra sugar is dissolved. Boil, uncovered, stirring occasionally, about 20 minutes or until jam jells when tested on a cold saucer. Pour hot jam into hot sterilised jars; seal immediately.

Makes about 1.5 litres (6 cups).

■ Storage: In cool, dark place for about 6 months; refrigerate after opening.

LEFT: Roasted Tomato Stock (in bottle); Traditional Tomato Paste (in top small jar); Tomato Pesto (in bowl and bottom jar). BELOW: From left: Rhubarb and Tomato Chutney; Fig, Tomato and Caramelised Onion Jam.

MANGO, APPLE AND TOMATO RELISH

2 large (400g) onions
8 medium (1.5kg) tomatoes
2 tablespoons olive oil
2 cloves garlic, crushed
1 cinnamon stick
2 teaspoons ground ginger
1 teaspoon ground turmeric
2 large (400g) apples, chopped
2 medium (860g) mangoes, chopped
1 cup (250ml) white wine vinegar
1 cup (200g) firmly packed
brown sugar
2 tablespoons seeded mustard
2 teaspoons salt

Cut onions and tomatoes into thin wedges. Heat oil in large pan, add onions and garlic, cook, stirring, until onions are soft. Add spices, cook, stirring, until fragrant. Add tomatoes with remaining ingredients, stir over heat, without boiling, until sugar is dissolved. Simmer, uncovered, stirring occasionally, about 1 hour or until mixture is thick. Discard cinnamon, pour hot relish into hot sterilised jars; seal immediately.

Makes about 2 litres (8 cups).

▨ Storage: Refrigerated for about 2 months.

SPICY ONION AND TOMATO RELISH

6 medium (1.1kg) tomatoes,
peeled, chopped
2 medium (300g) onions,
finely chopped
2 medium (300g) apples,
peeled, finely chopped
1 teaspoon salt
1 teaspoon grated lemon rind
1 teaspoon dry mustard
1 teaspoon garam masala
2 tablespoons mild curry powder
1¼ cups (250g) firmly packed
brown sugar
½ cup (125ml) white vinegar
¼ cup (60ml) lemon juice
1 tablespoon tomato paste

Combine all ingredients in large pan, simmer, uncovered, stirring occasionally, about 30 minutes or until mixture is thick. Pour hot relish into hot sterilised jars, seal immediately.

Makes about 1 litre (4 cups).

▨ Storage: Refrigerated for about 2 months.

Pewter bowls and spoon from Home & Garden on the Mall

From left: Spicy Onion and Tomato Relish; Mango, Apple and Tomato Relish.

TOMATO GINGER AND PASSIONFRUIT JAM

You will need about 10 passionfruit.

**4 large (1kg) tomatoes,
    peeled, chopped
1 large (200g) apple,
    peeled, chopped
1 cup (250ml) passionfruit pulp
4 cups (880g) sugar
½ cup (115g) glace ginger, chopped
½ cup (125ml) lemon juice**

Combine tomatoes with apple in large pan, simmer, uncovered, stirring occasionally, until apple is soft. Add remaining ingredients, stir over heat, without boiling, until sugar is dissolved. Simmer, uncovered, without stirring, about 35 minutes or until mixture jells when tested on a cold saucer. Pour hot jam into hot sterilised jars; seal immediately.

Makes about 1.25 litres (5 cups).

■ Storage: In cool, dark place for about 6 months; refrigerate after opening.

TOMATO NECTARINE JAM

**2 medium (280g) lemons
2 large (600g) oranges
6 large (1.5kg) tomatoes, peeled,
    seeded, chopped
10 medium (1.5kg) nectarines,
    peeled, chopped
4½ cups (1kg) sugar, approximately
2 tablespoons brandy**

Squeeze juice from lemons; discard rind, reserve seeds. You need ½ cup (125ml) lemon juice. Discard rind and pith from oranges; chop flesh roughly, reserve seeds. Tie all seeds in a piece of muslin. Combine lemon juice, orange flesh, muslin bag, tomatoes and nectarines in large pan, simmer, covered, about 45 minutes or until nectarines are very soft; discard muslin bag.

Measure fruit mixture, allow ¾ cup (165g) sugar to each cup of fruit mixture. Return fruit mixture with sugar to pan, stir over heat, without boiling, until sugar is dissolved. Boil, uncovered, stirring occasionally, about 15 minutes or until jam jells when tested on a cold saucer. Skim surface; stir in brandy. Stand 5 minutes then pour hot jam into hot sterilised jars; seal immediately.

Makes about 1.75 litres (7 cups).

■ Storage: In cool, dark place for about 6 months; refrigerate after opening.

ABOVE: From left: Tomato, Ginger and Passionfruit Jam; Tomato Nectarine Jam.

GREEN TOMATO SAUCE

Use in a similar way to tomato sauce.

1 tablespoon olive oil
1 large (200g) onion, chopped
1 clove garlic, chopped
2 teaspoons grated fresh ginger
3 teaspoons ground cumin
2 teaspoons ground coriander
1/4 teaspoon ground cinnamon
2 teaspoons ground turmeric
6 large (1.5kg) green tomatoes, chopped
3/4 cup (180ml) water
1 teaspoon salt
1 cup (250ml) white wine vinegar
1 cup (200g) firmly packed brown sugar

Heat oil in large pan, add onion, garlic, ginger and spices, cook, stirring, until onion is soft. Add tomatoes and water, simmer, covered, stirring occasionally, about 30 minutes or until tomatoes are pulpy. Blend or process mixture in batches until smooth, return to pan. Stir in remaining ingredients, stir over heat, without boiling, until sugar is dissolved. Simmer, uncovered, stirring occasionally, about 30 minutes or until thickened. Pour hot sauce into hot sterilised bottles; seal immediately.

Makes about 1 litre (4 cups).

■ Storage: In cool, dark place for about 6 months; refrigerate after opening.

◘ TOMATO, RED WINE AND ROSEMARY SAUCE

Suitable for steak, chops and barbecued meat.

1 tablespoon olive oil
1 large (200g) onion, finely chopped
1 small (70g) carrot, finely chopped
1 clove garlic, crushed
6 medium (1.1kg) tomatoes, chopped
1 1/4 cups (310ml) dry red wine
1 cup (250ml) beef stock
3 sprigs fresh rosemary
1 bay leaf

Heat oil in large pan, add onion, carrot and garlic, cook, stirring, about 10 minutes or until onion is lightly browned. Add remaining ingredients, simmer, uncovered, stirring occasionally, about 30 minutes or until reduced by half. Press mixture through fine sieve, discard pulp. Pour hot sauce into hot sterilised jar; seal immediately.

Makes about 625ml (2 1/2 cups).

■ Storage: Refrigerated for about 1 week.

RIGHT: Clockwise from front left: Green Tomato Sauce; Tomato Cranberry Ketchup; Tomato, Red Wine and Rosemary Sauce.

TOMATO CRANBERRY KETCHUP

1 tablespoon olive oil
2 medium (300g) onions, chopped
2 cloves garlic, crushed
1 tablespoon grated fresh ginger
1 tablespoon ground cumin
2 teaspoons ground coriander
2 teaspoons ground black pepper
10 medium (1.9kg) tomatoes, peeled, chopped
500g frozen cranberries
1 teaspoon salt
1/2 cup (100g) firmly packed brown sugar
1/2 cup (125ml) brown vinegar

Heat oil in pan, add onions, garlic, ginger and spices, cook, stirring, until onions are soft. Add remaining ingredients, stir over heat, without boiling, until sugar is dissolved. Simmer, uncovered, about 30 minutes or until mixture thickens. Push mixture through fine sieve, discard pulp. Pour hot ketchup into hot sterilised bottles; seal immediately.

Makes about 750ml (3 cups).

■ Storage: Refrigerated for about 6 weeks.

Sauce boat from Accoutrement

TOMATO AND CUCUMBER RELISH

3 teaspoons black mustard seeds
2 teaspoons ground allspice
1 teaspoon cayenne pepper
2 teaspoons salt
6 large (1.5kg) tomatoes, chopped
3 small (400g) Lebanese
  cucumbers, finely chopped
4 medium (800g) red peppers,
  finely chopped
4 sticks celery, finely chopped
1 large (200g) onion, finely chopped
1½ cups (375ml) cider vinegar
¾ cup (180ml) apple juice
1½ cups (300g) firmly packed
  brown sugar

Combine all ingredients in large pan, stir over heat, without boiling, until sugar is dissolved. Simmer, uncovered, stirring occasionally, about 1½ hours or until mixture is thick. Pour hot relish into hot sterilised jars; seal immediately.

Makes about 2 litres (8 cups).

■ Storage: Refrigerated for about 2 months.

HORSERADISH TOMATO SPREAD

Can be served as a dip or with barbecued meat.

6 large (1.5kg) tomatoes,
  peeled, chopped
2 medium (300g) onions,
  finely chopped
2 sticks celery, finely chopped
½ cup (125ml) tomato juice
1 cup (250ml) white vinegar
½ teaspoon ground black
  peppercorns
4 cloves
1 cinnamon stick
¾ cup (150g) firmly packed
  brown sugar
2 teaspoons horseradish relish
1 tablespoon Worcestershire sauce
1 tablespoon lemon juice
2 tablespoons drained, chopped
  sun-dried tomatoes in oil

Combine fresh tomatoes, onions, celery and juice in large pan, cook, stirring, about 10 minutes or until thick and pulpy. Combine vinegar, pepper, cloves and cinnamon in small pan, cover, slowly bring to boil; strain.

Add vinegar mixture with remaining ingredients to tomato mixture, stir over heat until sugar is dissolved. Simmer, uncovered, stirring occasionally, about 20 minutes or until thick. Blend or process mixture in batches until almost smooth; spoon hot spread into hot sterilised jars; seal immediately.

Makes about 1 litre (4 cups).

■ Storage: Refrigerated for about 2 months.

GREEN TOMATO PICKLES

⅔ cup (150g) coarse cooking salt
1.5 litres (6 cups) boiling water
5 medium (1kg) green tomatoes,
  peeled, sliced
1 large (200g) onion, sliced
2 large (600g) red Spanish
  onions, sliced
2 cups (440g) sugar
2 teaspoons finely chopped
  fresh ginger
2½ cups (625ml) white vinegar
1 medium (200g) red pepper,
  chopped
1 medium (200g) yellow pepper,
  chopped
1 teaspoon ground turmeric
1 teaspoon mild curry powder
1 teaspoon dry mustard
¼ teaspoon ground allspice
¼ teaspoon cayenne pepper
½ cup (75g) plain flour

Combine salt with water in large bowl, stir until salt is dissolved, add tomatoes and onions; mix gently. Cover, refrigerate overnight.

Drain tomato mixture, discard liquid. Combine sugar, ginger and 2 cups (500ml) of the vinegar in large pan, stir over heat, without boiling, until sugar is dissolved. Add tomato mixture and peppers, bring to boil. Blend remaining vinegar with spices and flour, stir into tomato mixture, stir over heat until mixture boils and thickens slightly. Simmer, uncovered, stirring often, about 30 minutes or until mixture is thick. Spoon hot pickles into hot sterilised jars; seal immediately.

Makes about 1.5 litres (6 cups).

■ Storage: Refrigerated for about 2 months.

Clockwise from left: Horseradish Tomato Spread; Tomato and Cucumber Relish; Green Tomato Pickles.

Platter, bowls and spoons from Accoutrement

MUSTARD SEED AND TOMATO SAUCE

2 tablespoons olive oil
1 small (80g) onion, finely chopped
2 cloves garlic, crushed
6 medium (450g) egg tomatoes, peeled, chopped
2 green shallots, chopped
½ cup (125ml) dry white wine
2 teaspoons salt
2 teaspoons brown sugar
2 teaspoons tomato paste
3 teaspoons seeded mustard

Heat oil in medium pan, add onion and garlic, cook, stirring, until onion is soft. Add tomatoes, cook until tomatoes are soft. Blend or process tomato mixture until smooth; strain through fine sieve, discard seeds. Return tomato mixture to same pan, add remaining ingredients. Boil, uncovered, about 5 minutes or until sauce thickens slightly. Pour sauce into hot sterilised bottles; seal immediately.

Makes about 375ml (1½ cups).

■ Storage: Refrigerated for about 6 months.

ORANGE AND TOMATO SALSA

The light, fresh flavours are ideal for chicken or fish kebabs.

3 large (900g) oranges
4 medium (760g) tomatoes, seeded, chopped
1 teaspoon grated fresh ginger
2 tablespoons chopped fresh coriander leaves
½ teaspoon sesame oil
½ teaspoon chilli oil
1 clove garlic, crushed
1 tablespoon lime juice

Peel oranges thickly; discard seeds and pith. Cut between membranes into segments; chop orange segments.

Combine all ingredients in medium bowl, cover, refrigerate at least 1 hour before using.

Makes about 500ml (2 cups).

■ Storage: Covered, in refrigerator; use within 2 days.

SWEET CHILLI TOMATO SAUCE

4 large (1kg) tomatoes, chopped
1 teaspoon salt
4 cloves garlic, chopped
¼ cup (60ml) balsamic vinegar
¼ cup (55g) sugar
¼ cup chopped fresh coriander leaves
3 small fresh red chillies, chopped

Combine all ingredients in large pan, stir over heat, without boiling, until sugar is dissolved. Simmer, uncovered, stirring occasionally, about 20 minutes or until sauce thickens; cool 5 minutes. Blend or process sauce until smooth. Pour hot sauce into hot sterilised bottles, seal immediately.

Makes about 625ml (2½ cups).

■ Storage: Refrigerated for about 2 weeks.

Tiles from Country Floors

Canisters and spoon from Home & Garden on the Mall; placemat from Accoutrement

FIG, DATE AND TOMATO RELISH

8 medium (1.5kg) tomatoes, peeled, chopped
2 medium (300g) apples, peeled, chopped
2 medium (300g) onions, chopped
1 cup (160g) sultanas
1/2 cup (80g) chopped seeded dates
1/2 cup (95g) chopped dried figs
2 teaspoons salt
4 cloves garlic, thinly sliced
2 teaspoons ground cumin
1/4 cup firmly packed fresh mint leaves
1/3 cup (80ml) lime juice
2 cups (500ml) brown vinegar
2 1/2 cups (500g) firmly packed brown sugar

Combine all ingredients in large pan, stir over heat, without boiling, until sugar is dissolved. Simmer, uncovered, stirring occasionally, about 1 hour or until mixture thickens. Spoon hot relish into hot sterilised jars; seal immediately.

Makes about 2 litres (8 cups).

■ Storage: Refrigerated for about 2 months.

PEPPER, PEAR AND TOMATO CHUTNEY

2 large (700g) yellow peppers, chopped
1.3kg yellow teardrop tomatoes, halved
2 teaspoons salt
2 tablespoons ground cumin
1 tablespoon ground turmeric
1 tablespoon mild curry powder
1 tablespoon ground coriander
1/3 cup (65g) yellow mustard seeds
1 tablespoon grated fresh ginger
5 cloves garlic, crushed
2 medium (300g) onions, chopped
2 cups (400g) firmly packed brown sugar
2 1/2 cups (625ml) cider vinegar
1 1/2 cups (225g) chopped dried pears

Combine all ingredients in large pan, stir over heat, without boiling, until sugar is dissolved. Simmer, uncovered, stirring occasionally, about 45 minutes or until mixture has thickened. Spoon hot chutney into hot sterilised jars; seal immediately.

Makes about 1.75 litres (7 cups).

■ Storage: Refrigerated for about 6 months.

LEFT: From left: Mustard Seed and Tomato Sauce; Orange and Tomato Salsa; Sweet Chilli Tomato Sauce.
ABOVE: From left: Pepper, Pear and Tomato Chutney; Fig, Date and Tomato Relish.

OVEN-DRIED EGG TOMATOES IN HERBED OIL

It is important for preservation that the tomatoes be dried thoroughly and evenly. Garlic and herbs must be dried until crisp.

30 small (1.8kg) egg tomatoes
4 cloves garlic, thinly sliced
6 fresh basil leaves
4 sprigs fresh thyme
6 fresh sage leaves
2 tablespoons fine sea salt
2 cups (500ml) olive oil,
    approximately

Cut tomatoes in half lengthways. Place garlic and herbs, and tomatoes, cut side up, on wire racks over oven trays. Sprinkle tomatoes with salt. Bake in very slow oven 6 to 8 hours or until tomatoes are dry. Herbs will take about 20 minutes to dry; garlic about 30 minutes. Herbs and garlic must be dried until crisp. Turn and rearrange tomatoes several times during drying. Pack tomatoes, garlic and herbs into sterilised jar (1 litre/4 cup capacity). Pour in enough oil to cover tomatoes completely; seal immediately.

■ Storage: Up to about 6 months in cool, dark place.

SUN-DRIED TOMATO CHUTNEY

3 cups (180g) sun-dried tomatoes
1 tablespoon olive oil
2 medium (300g) onions, chopped
2 teaspoons grated fresh ginger
3 teaspoons black mustard seeds
2 teaspoons mixed spice
3 medium (450g) apples, peeled,
    finely chopped
1 cup (160g) sultanas
1 cup (200g) firmly packed
    brown sugar
2 cups (500ml) apple juice
1 cup (250ml) balsamic vinegar
½ cup (125ml) cider vinegar
⅓ cup (80ml) water
¼ cup (60ml) lemon juice
1 teaspoon salt

Place tomatoes in medium bowl, cover with boiling water, stand about 5 minutes or until soft. Drain tomatoes; roughly chop. Heat oil in large pan, add onions, ginger, seeds and spice, cook, stirring, until onions are soft. Add tomatoes and remaining ingredients, stir over heat, without boiling, until sugar is dissolved. Simmer, uncovered, stirring occasionally, about 50 minutes or until mixture is thick. Spoon hot chutney into hot sterilised jars; seal immediately.

Makes about 1.5 litres (6 cups).

■ Storage: In cool, dark place for about 6 months; refrigerate after opening.

From left: Oven-Dried Egg Tomatoes in Herbed Oil; Sun-Dried Tomato Chutney.

Oil bottle from The Bay Tree Kitchen Shop; stainless steel bowl from Accoutrement

BASIC TOMATO KETCHUP

1 teaspoon black peppercorns
6 cloves
1 bay leaf
8 large (2kg) tomatoes, chopped
2 medium (300g) onions, chopped
½ cup (125ml) red wine vinegar
1 cup (220g) sugar
2 teaspoons salt
1 tablespoon tomato paste

Tie peppercorns, cloves and bay leaf in piece of muslin. Place muslin bag in large pan with tomatoes and onions, simmer, uncovered, stirring occasionally, about 45 minutes or until onions are soft; discard bag. Cool mixture 10 minutes. Blend or process mixture until smooth; strain through fine sieve back into same pan. Add remaining ingredients, stir over heat, without boiling, until sugar is dissolved. Simmer, uncovered, stirring occasionally, about 15 minutes or until mixture thickens to desired pouring consistency. Pour hot ketchup into hot sterilised bottles; seal immediately.

Makes about 1.25 litres (5 cups).

■ Storage: In cool, dark place for about 6 months; refrigerate after opening.

TOMATO STRAWBERRY JAM

This is a soft-setting jam.

13 medium (2.5kg) tomatoes,
**   peeled, chopped**
750g strawberries, halved
¾ cup (180ml) lemon juice
6 cups (1.3kg) sugar, approximately

Combine tomatoes, strawberries and juice in large pan, boil, uncovered, stirring occasionally, about 40 minutes or until tomatoes are pulpy.

Measure fruit mixture, allow ¾ cup (165g) sugar to each cup of fruit mixture. Return fruit mixture with sugar to pan, stir over heat, without boiling, until sugar is dissolved. Boil, uncovered, stirring occasionally, about 20 minutes or until jam jells when tested on a cold saucer. Pour hot jam into hot sterilised jars; seal immediately.

Makes about 2 litres (8 cups).

■ Storage: In cool, dark place for about 6 months; refrigerate after opening.

LEFT: Tomato Strawberry Jam.
RIGHT: Basic Tomato Ketchup.

Tomato separator from The Bay Tree Kitchen Shop; tray from Ventura Design

TOMATO HERB VINEGAR

Use in dressings in place of usual vinegars.

½ teaspoon black peppercorns
1 teaspoon coriander seeds
1 teaspoon cumin seeds
2 cloves garlic, crushed
1 cup (250ml) tomato juice
2 cups (500ml) white vinegar
2 teaspoons brown sugar
1 tablespoon drained, chopped
    sun-dried tomatoes in oil
4 sprigs fresh thyme

Lightly crush peppercorns and seeds, place in small pan, stir over heat until fragrant, remove from pan; cool. Combine garlic and juice in same pan, simmer, uncovered, until mixture is reduced to ½ cup (125ml). Combine seed mixture with tomato mixture, vinegar, sugar and sun-dried tomatoes in bowl. Wash thyme sprigs, pat dry, add to vinegar mixture. Cover, refrigerate 3 days. Pour vinegar mixture into hot sterilised bottles; seal immediately.

Makes about 500ml (2 cups).

■ Storage: Refrigerated for about
   2 weeks.

TOMATO TARRAGON DRESSING

Use as a salad dressing.

3 small (390g) tomatoes,
   peeled, chopped
1 clove garlic, chopped
2 tablespoons white wine vinegar
2 teaspoons Dijon mustard
¼ teaspoon cracked black
   peppercorns
½ teaspoon sugar
¼ teaspoon salt
½ cup (125ml) olive oil
1½ tablespoons chopped
   fresh tarragon

Blend or process tomatoes, garlic, vinegar, mustard, pepper, sugar and salt until smooth. Add oil gradually in a thin stream while motor is operating. Stir in tarragon. Stir in a little water to give desired consistency, if necessary. Pour dressing into cold sterilised bottles; seal immediately.

Makes about 500ml (2 cups).

■ Storage: Refrigerated for about
   1 week.

ROASTED ONION, GARLIC AND TOMATO MAYONNAISE

3 medium (450g) onions
1 large (100g) garlic bulb
2 egg yolks
1 tablespoon lemon juice
¼ teaspoon salt
2 teaspoons Dijon mustard
1 cup (250ml) olive oil
½ cup (75g) drained, chopped
   sun-dried tomatoes in oil
2 tablespoons chopped fresh chives

Place unpeeled onions in baking dish, bake, uncovered, in moderate oven 30 minutes. Wrap garlic in foil, place in baking dish with onions, bake about 30 minutes or until onions and garlic are soft; cool.

Remove skin from onions and garlic. Blend or process onions, garlic, egg yolks, juice, salt and mustard until smooth. Add oil gradually in a thin stream while motor is operating, blend until thick. Add tomatoes and chives, blend until combined. Stir in a little water to give desired consistency, if necessary. Pour into cold sterilised jars; seal immediately.

Makes about 375ml (1½ cups).

■ Storage: Refrigerated for about
   1 week.

Tiles from Country Floors; porcelain spoon from The Bay Tree Kitchen Shop

From left: Tomato Tarragon Dressing; Roasted Onion, Garlic and Tomato Mayonnaise; Tomato Herb Vinegar.

CITRUS, TOMATO AND BEETROOT CHUTNEY

1 medium (140g) lemon
1 large (300g) orange
4 large (1kg) tomatoes, chopped
3 medium (480g) beetroot, peeled, chopped
2 medium (300g) onions, chopped
1½ cups (375ml) brown vinegar
2 cups (400g) firmly packed brown sugar
1 cup (150g) dried currants
1 teaspoon black peppercorns
2 teaspoons ground ginger
2 teaspoons ground coriander
1 teaspoon ground cinnamon
¾ cup (180ml) water

Cut unpeeled lemon and orange into quarters, slice thinly; discard seeds. Place lemon, orange, tomatoes and beetroot in large pan, add just enough water to cover, simmer, covered, about 30 minutes or until rind is very soft; drain. Combine mixture with remaining ingredients in large pan, stir over heat, without boiling, until sugar is dissolved. Simmer, uncovered, stirring occasionally, about 50 minutes or until chutney is as thick as desired. Spoon hot chutney into hot sterilised jars; seal immediately.

Makes about 1.5 litres (6 cups).

■ Storage: In cool, dark place for about 6 months; refrigerate after opening.

◧ ROASTED PEPPER AND TOMATO SAUCE

8 large (2kg) tomatoes, quartered
2 large (600g) red Spanish onions, chopped
5 cloves garlic, peeled
2 sticks celery, chopped
½ cup firmly packed fresh basil leaves
½ cup (125ml) red wine vinegar
¼ cup (60ml) olive oil
¼ cup (50g) brown sugar
2 teaspoons cumin seeds
1½ teaspoons ground hot paprika
1 teaspoon cracked black peppercorns
1 teaspoon salt
4 large (1.4kg) red peppers

Combine tomatoes, onions, garlic, celery, basil, vinegar, oil, sugar, spices, black pepper and salt in large baking dish. Bake, uncovered, in hot oven, stirring occasionally, about 1 hour or until tomatoes are pulpy.

Meanwhile, quarter red peppers, remove seeds and membranes. Grill peppers, skin side up, until skin blisters and blackens. Peel away skin, chop peppers. Blend or process peppers and tomato mixture in batches until almost smooth; strain; discard pulp. Pour hot sauce into hot sterilised bottles; seal immediately.

Makes about 2 litres (8 cups).

■ Storage: Refrigerated for about 6 weeks.

◧ FRESH TOMATO PASTA SAUCE

2 tablespoons olive oil
1 large (200g) onion, chopped
2 cloves garlic, crushed
10 medium (1.9kg) tomatoes, peeled, chopped
2 teaspoons salt
½ cup (125ml) dry red wine
2 teaspoons brown sugar
2 tablespoons tomato paste
2 tablespoons finely chopped fresh basil
2 tablespoons finely chopped fresh parsley
2 teaspoons finely chopped fresh oregano leaves
½ teaspoon cracked black peppercorns

Heat oil in pan, add onion and garlic, cook, stirring, until onion is soft. Add tomatoes, salt and wine, simmer, uncovered, about 15 minutes or until tomatoes are soft.

Add remaining ingredients, simmer, uncovered, about 10 minutes or until thickened. Pour hot sauce into hot sterilised bottles; seal immediately.

Makes about 1.5 litres (6 cups).

■ Storage: Refrigerated for about 3 days.

LEFT: From left: Citrus, Tomato and Beetroot Chutney; Roasted Pepper and Tomato Sauce.
RIGHT: Fresh Tomato Pasta Sauce.

Tiles from Country Floors

FIERY CHILLI TOMATO CHUTNEY

8 medium (1.5kg) tomatoes,
    peeled, seeded, chopped
1 large (200g) onion, chopped
4 cloves garlic, crushed
1 medium (200g) red pepper,
    chopped
2 teaspoons grated fresh ginger
2 cups (500ml) cider vinegar
2 cups (440g) sugar
½ cup (125ml) lemon juice
1 cup (160g) sultanas
2 teaspoons salt
1 cinnamon stick
6 cloves
5 small fresh red chillies,
    finely chopped
2 teaspoons chilli powder

Combine tomatoes with onion, garlic, pepper and ginger in large pan. Simmer, uncovered, stirring occasionally, about 15 minutes or until onion is soft. Add remaining ingredients, stir over heat, without boiling, until sugar is dissolved. Simmer, uncovered, stirring occasionally, about 1 hour or until mixture thickens. Discard cinnamon. Spoon hot chutney into hot sterilised jars; seal immediately.

Makes about 1.5 litres (6 cups).

■ Storage: In cool, dark place for
    about 6 months; refrigerate
    after opening.

SUN-DRIED TOMATO AND OLIVE TAPENADE

1 cup (150g) drained sun-dried
    tomatoes in oil
1 tablespoon olive oil
1 tablespoon red wine vinegar
1 tablespoon brown sugar
1 tablespoon chopped fresh
    oregano leaves
1 tablespoon chopped fresh basil
½ teaspoon cracked black
    peppercorns
2/3 cup (70g) pecans, toasted
1/3 cup (50g) seeded black olives

Process all ingredients until smooth. Spoon tapenade into cold sterilised jars; seal immediately.

Makes about 2 cups (500ml).

■ Storage: Refrigerated for about
    6 weeks.

Tray from Ventura Design

From left: Sun-Dried Tomato and Olive Tapenade; Fiery Chilli Tomato Chutney.

23

TOMATO BASIL OIL

Use combined with vinegar to make a dressing.

8 medium (1.5kg) tomatoes, chopped
1/4 cup fresh basil leaves
1/2 teaspoon salt
1/2 teaspoon cracked black peppercorns
1/2 cup (125ml) olive oil

Extract juice from tomatoes, using a vegetable juice extractor; discard pulp. You need 4 cups (1 litre) of juice.

Transfer juice to medium pan, simmer, uncovered, about 20 minutes or until reduced to 2 1/2 cups (625ml), cool 10 minutes. Strain tomato mixture through fine sieve, return to pan with basil, salt and pepper. Boil, uncovered, stirring occasionally, about 20 minutes or until sauce thickens; discard basil. Stir in oil, reheat, pour into hot sterilised bottles; seal immediately.

Makes about 500ml (2 cups).

■ Storage: Refrigerated for about 1 month; shake well before using.

ROASTED TOMATO AIOLI

Good with vegetables or seafood.

4 large (360g) egg tomatoes, quartered
1 tablespoon olive oil
1 teaspoon salt
1 small clove garlic, chopped
1 tablespoon lemon juice
1 tablespoon white wine vinegar
2 egg yolks
1/2 cup (125ml) vegetable oil
1/2 cup (125ml) olive oil, extra
1 tablespoon chopped fresh thyme

Place tomatoes, cut side up, on wire rack over baking dish, drizzle with olive oil, sprinkle with salt. Bake in moderate oven about 1 hour or until tomatoes are very soft; cool. Blend or process tomatoes, garlic, juice, vinegar and egg yolks until smooth. Add combined vegetable and extra olive oil gradually in a thin stream while motor is operating, blend until thick. Stir in thyme. Pour into cold sterilised jars; seal immediately.

Makes about 500ml (2 cups).

■ Storage: Refrigerated for about 1 week.

F SPICY BARBECUE MARINADE

Perfect for beef steaks. If using as a sauce after marinating, bring remaining marinade to boil, simmer few minutes before using.

1 large (200g) onion, chopped
425g can tomatoes
3 cloves garlic, crushed
1/3 cup (80ml) cider vinegar
1/4 cup (60ml) Worcestershire sauce
1/2 teaspoon ground coriander
1/2 teaspoon ground cumin
1/2 teaspoon chilli powder
1/2 teaspoon ground black peppercorns
1 tablespoon brown sugar
1/4 cup (60ml) olive oil

Blend or process onion and undrained tomatoes until finely chopped. Add remaining ingredients, blend until combined. Pour mixture into medium pan, simmer, uncovered, about 5 minutes or until mixture thickens slightly. Pour hot marinade into hot sterilised jars; seal immediately.

Makes about 625ml (2 1/2 cups).

■ Storage: Refrigerated for about 1 month.

F TOMATO AND JALAPENO PEPPER MARINADE

Best with seafood or chicken.

5 large (450g) egg tomatoes, quartered
1 medium (150g) onion, chopped
1/4 cup (50g) drained, bottled chopped jalapeno peppers
4 cloves garlic, peeled, chopped
2 teaspoons ground cumin
1/4 cup fresh oregano leaves
2 tablespoons brown vinegar
2 tablespoons brown sugar
2 tablespoons olive oil

Blend or process all ingredients until smooth. Pour marinade into cold sterilised bottles; seal immediately.

Makes about (625ml) 2 1/2 cups.

■ Storage: Refrigerated for about 2 weeks.

Tiles from Country Floors; wooden spoon from The Bay Tree Kitchen Shop

LEFT: From left: Roasted Tomato Aioli; Tomato Basil Oil.
RIGHT: From left: Spicy Barbecue Marinade; Tomato and Jalapeno Pepper Marinade.

◨ PLUM AND PORT SAUCE

Delicious with beef, pork and game.

1 tablespoon olive oil
2 medium (300g) onions, chopped
3 cloves garlic, crushed
¼ cup (60ml) red wine vinegar
¼ cup (50g) brown sugar
½ teaspoon salt
8 medium (1.5kg) tomatoes, peeled, chopped
6 medium (780g) blood plums, peeled, seeded, chopped
1 cup (250ml) port
2 teaspoons juniper berries

Heat oil in large pan, add onions and garlic, cook, stirring, until onions are soft. Add remaining ingredients, stir over heat, without boiling, until sugar is dissolved. Simmer, uncovered, stirring occasionally, about 30 minutes or until sauce has thickened. Blend or process mixture until finely chopped, strain; discard pulp. Pour hot sauce into hot sterilised bottles, seal immediately.

Makes about 1 litre (4 cups).

■ Storage: Refrigerated for about 2 weeks.

BOTTLED ANTIPASTO

Can be eaten immediately.

2 medium (400g) red peppers
1 medium (200g) yellow pepper
3 medium (360g) zucchini
4 (240g) finger eggplants
4 large (1kg) tomatoes
1 tablespoon dried thyme leaves
1 tablespoon fine sea salt
1 teaspoon ground black peppercorns
½ cup (125ml) vegetable oil
1¼ cups (310ml) olive oil
2 tablespoons balsamic vinegar

Quarter peppers, remove seeds and membranes. Grill peppers, skin side up, until skin blisters and blackens. Peel away skin, slice peppers thickly. Cut zucchini and eggplants lengthways into 5mm slices. Trim tomatoes at both ends, cut in half.

Cook zucchini and eggplants in batches in heated greased griddle pan (or grill or barbecue) until browned and tender. Cook tomatoes in batches in same pan until browned and just tender. Pack hot vegetables and tomatoes into wide-necked, hot sterilised jar (1.5 litre/6 cup capacity).

Combine thyme, salt, pepper and oils in small pan, stir until hot. Remove from heat, carefully add vinegar. Pour enough oil mixture into jar to cover vegetable mixture completely; seal immediately. Invert jar every few days.

■ Storage: Refrigerated for about 2 weeks.

LEFT: Plum and Port Sauce.
RIGHT: Bottled Antipasto.

Tray from Ventura Design

Spoon from Home & Garden on the Mall

TOMATO, EGGPLANT AND PEPPER RELISH

2 small (460g) eggplants
coarse cooking salt
3 medium (600g) red peppers
2 tablespoons olive oil
1 large (200g) onion, sliced
1 clove garlic, crushed
2 teaspoons black mustard seeds
3 teaspoons cumin seeds
1/4 teaspoon cardamom seeds
6 medium (1.1kg) tomatoes, peeled,
    seeded, chopped
3/4 cup (180ml) white wine vinegar
1/4 cup (60ml) red wine vinegar
1 tablespoon balsamic vinegar
1/3 cup (65g) firmly packed
    brown sugar

Slice eggplants, place in strainer, sprinkle with salt, stand 30 minutes. Rinse slices under cold water; drain on absorbent paper. Chop eggplant slices. Quarter peppers, remove seeds and membranes. Grill peppers, skin side up, until skin blisters and blackens. Peel away skin, chop peppers.

Heat oil in large pan, add onion, garlic and seeds, cook, stirring, until onion is soft. Add eggplants, cook, stirring, until lightly browned. Add peppers with remaining ingredients, simmer, covered, stirring occasionally, 50 minutes. Remove lid, simmer about 10 minutes or until mixture is thick. Pour hot relish into hot sterilised jars; seal immediately.

Makes about 1 litre (4 cups).

▨ Storage: Refrigerated for about
    1 month.

GREEN TOMATO AND PEAR CHUTNEY

4 small (720g) under-ripe pears,
    peeled, chopped
7 medium (1.3kg) under-ripe
    tomatoes, chopped
2 large (400g) onions, chopped
1 cup (150g) dried currants
1/4 cup (45g) black mustard seeds
2 cups (500ml) brown vinegar
2 cups (400g) firmly packed
    brown sugar
2 teaspoons salt
1 tablespoon ground coriander
1 tablespoon ground ginger
2 teaspoons ground cardamom

Combine all ingredients in large pan, stir over heat, without boiling, until sugar is dissolved. Simmer, uncovered, stirring occasionally, about 1 hour or until thick. Spoon hot chutney into hot sterilised jars; seal immediately.

Makes about 1.75 litres (7 cups).

▨ Storage: In cool, dark place for about
    6 months; refrigerate after opening.

From left: Green Tomato and Pear Chutney; Tomato, Eggplant and Pepper Relish.

Hand-made ceramics by Anna Paola

Wire stand from Accoutrement

CHERRY TOMATOES WITH OLIVES

Marinated green olives are available in several different flavours; use your favourite in this recipe.

750g cherry tomatoes, halved
2 tablespoons fine sea salt
3/4 cup (120g) marinated
green olives
3/4 cup (120g) seeded black olives
1½ cups (375ml) olive oil,
approximately

Place tomatoes, cut side up, on wire racks over oven trays; sprinkle with salt. Bake in very slow oven about 4 hours or until tomatoes are dry. Turn and rearrange tomatoes frequently while drying. Pack hot tomatoes and olives into hot sterilised jar (3 cup/750ml capacity). Pour in enough oil to cover tomatoes and olives; seal immediately.

Makes about 750ml (3 cups).

■ Storage: Refrigerated for about 1 month.

SPICY MARINATED TOMATOES AND FETA CHEESE

6 cloves garlic, thinly sliced
6 sprigs fresh thyme
3½ cups (875ml) olive oil
8 cardamom pods
10 small dried red chillies
1 cinnamon stick
3 dried kaffir lime leaves
1 teaspoon cumin seeds
1 teaspoon mild curry powder
3 cups (180g) sun-dried tomatoes
300g feta cheese, chopped

Place garlic and thyme sprigs on wire rack over oven tray. Bake in very slow oven about 30 minutes or until garlic is dry and crisp. Thyme will take about 20 minutes to become dry and crisp.

Heat 1 tablespoon of the oil in small pan, add cardamom pods, chillies, cinnamon, lime leaves, seeds and curry powder, cook, stirring, until fragrant. Combine spice mixture with garlic, thyme and remaining oil in large jug. Place tomatoes in large bowl, cover with boiling water, stand about 5 minutes or until softened; drain. Gently pat tomatoes dry with absorbent paper.

Layer tomatoes and cheese in cold sterilised jars (1.5 litre/6 cup capacity). Pour in enough oil mixture to cover tomatoes and feta completely; seal immediately.

■ Storage: Refrigerated for about 2 weeks.

ABOVE: From left: Cherry Tomatoes with Olives; Spicy Marinated Tomatoes and Feta Cheese.

Plate and server from Ventura Design

PICKLED GREEN TOMATOES

8 medium (1.5kg) green tomatoes, quartered
1 litre (4 cups) white vinegar
1 cup (250ml) white wine vinegar
2 cloves garlic, sliced
2 cinnamon sticks
4 bay leaves
1/4 cup (55g) fine sea salt
1 tablespoon black peppercorns
1 teaspoon cloves

Pack tomatoes into hot sterilised jars (9 cup/2.25 litre capacity). Combine remaining ingredients in large pan, simmer, uncovered, 15 minutes. Add enough vinegar mixture to jar to cover tomatoes completely; seal immediately.

■ Storage: Refrigerated for 6 weeks before opening.

RATATOUILLE CHUTNEY

2 medium (400g) red peppers
2 medium (400g) yellow peppers
2 tablespoons olive oil
2 medium (300g) onions, chopped
2 cloves garlic, crushed
2 small (460g) eggplants, chopped
1kg cherry tomatoes, chopped
660g yellow teardrop tomatoes, chopped
2 teaspoons salt
1/3 cup chopped fresh basil
2 tablespoons chopped fresh oregano leaves
1 1/2 cups (375ml) red wine vinegar
1 1/4 cups (275g) sugar
2 tablespoons drained capers, rinsed, chopped

Quarter peppers, remove seeds and membranes. Grill peppers, skin side up, until skin blisters and blackens. Peel away skin, chop peppers. Heat oil in large pan, add onions, garlic and eggplants, cook, stirring, until eggplants are browned. Add peppers with remaining ingredients, stir over heat, without boiling, until sugar is dissolved. Simmer, uncovered, stirring occasionally, about 1 1/4 hours or until mixture is thick. Spoon hot chutney into hot sterilised jars; seal immediately.

Makes about 1.5 litres (6 cups).

■ Storage: In cool, dark place for about 6 months; refrigerate after opening.

BELOW: From left at front: Ratatouille Chutney; Pickled Green Tomatoes.

ⓕ SPICED TOMATO PUREE

1 tablespoon olive oil
1 large (200g) onion, chopped
2 cloves garlic, chopped
2 small fresh red chillies, chopped
2 tablespoons chopped fresh basil
1 tablespoon tomato paste
1 teaspoon salt
2 tablespoons dry red wine
¼ cup (60ml) water
5 medium (1kg) tomatoes, peeled, seeded, chopped

Heat oil in large pan, add onion, garlic and chillies, cook, stirring, until onion is soft. Add remaining ingredients, simmer, uncovered, about 20 minutes, stirring occasionally, or until slightly thickened. Blend or process mixture in batches until smooth. Pour hot puree into hot sterilised jars; seal immediately.

Makes about 625ml (2½ cups).

■ Storage: Refrigerated for about 1 week.

TOMATO CURRY PASTE

5 small dried red chillies, chopped
1 tablespoon cumin seeds
1 tablespoon coriander seeds
4 cardamom pods
1 tablespoon garam masala
1 tablespoon ground turmeric
¼ cup (60ml) peanut oil
1 large (200g) onion, finely chopped
5 cloves garlic, crushed
2 tablespoons finely chopped fresh ginger
⅓ cup (80ml) tomato paste
¼ cup (35g) drained, chopped sun-dried tomatoes in oil
4 medium (760g) tomatoes, peeled, chopped
400g can coconut cream
1 tablespoon brown sugar
1 cinnamon stick
8 fresh curry leaves
8 fresh kaffir lime leaves
2 tablespoons fish sauce
¼ cup firmly packed fresh coriander leaves, chopped

Crush chillies, seeds and cardamom; stir in ground spices. Heat oil in large pan, add onion, garlic and ginger, cook, stirring, until onion is soft. Add chilli mixture, cook, stirring, until fragrant. Stir in paste and both tomatoes, cook, stirring, 2 minutes. Add coconut cream, sugar, cinnamon and curry and lime leaves, simmer, uncovered, stirring occasionally, about 30 minutes or until mixture thickens. Stir in sauce, then coriander. Spoon hot paste into hot sterilised jars; seal immediately.

Makes about 1.25 litres (5 cups).

■ Storage: Refrigerated for about 3 months.

From left: Tomato Curry Paste; Spiced Tomato Puree.

Strainer, saucepan and wire stand from Accoutrement

33

SUGARED EGG TOMATOES

These are delicious with cheese.

22 large (2kg) firm egg tomatoes
3 cups (750ml) water
3 cups (660g) sugar
2 tablespoons lemon juice
1 tablespoon glucose syrup
1 cinnamon stick
4 cloves
2 cups (320g) pure icing sugar,
**   approximately**

Peel tomatoes, halve lengthways. Combine water, sugar, juice, glucose, cinnamon and cloves in large pan, stir over heat, without boiling, until sugar is dissolved. Bring to boil, add tomatoes, simmer gently about 5 minutes or until tomatoes are slightly softened; stir gently once during cooking time. Drain tomatoes from the sugar syrup; reserve 2 cups (500ml) of the syrup.

Place tomatoes, cut side up, on fine wire racks over oven trays. Place reserved syrup in small pan, simmer, uncovered, about 10 minutes or until syrup thickens slightly.

Bake tomatoes, uncovered, in very slow oven, brushing with syrup every 30 minutes or until tomatoes are dry and well glazed. Tomatoes will take about 5 hours to reach this stage. Turn and rearrange tomatoes frequently during the drying process.

Cool on racks. Layer tomatoes in airtight containers, sifting plenty of icing sugar between the layers. Just before serving, sprinkle with more icing sugar.

■ Storage: In airtight container at room temperature.

TOMATO, APPLE AND GINGER FRUIT MINCE

Ideal with cold meat or curries.

4 small (520g) green tomatoes,
**   coarsely grated**
2 medium (300g) apples,
**   peeled, coarsely grated**
1 large (330g) firm pear,
**   peeled, coarsely grated**
1/2 cup (115g) glace ginger, chopped
2 teaspoons grated orange rind
2 teaspoons grated lemon rind
1/4 cup (50g) brown sugar
1 teaspoon mixed spice
1 tablespoon brandy
1 1/2 cups (255g) raisins, chopped
1 1/2 cups (240g) sultanas

Combine all ingredients in large bowl; mix well. Spoon mixture into cold sterilised jars; seal immediately. Invert jars every few days.

Makes about 2 litres (8 cups).

■ Storage: Refrigerated for about 3 months.

BOTTLED TOMATOES

We give different methods for bottling tomatoes; all are good. Use bottled tomatoes similar to canned tomatoes.

OVEN METHOD
16 small (1.5kg) tomatoes, peeled
3 cups (750ml) tomato juice
1/2 teaspoon salt
1 teaspoon sugar

Pack tomatoes into 2 hot sterilised preserving jars (1 litre/4 cup capacity each), fitted with rubber rings. Combine juice, salt and sugar in medium pan, bring to boil. Slowly pour boiling juice over tomatoes until jars are filled to within 1cm from top; seal immediately with lids and clips. Place jars, not touching, in baking dish, add enough boiling water to come 3cm up sides of jars. Stand in very slow oven for 1 hour. Remove jars carefully from dish; cool. Stand 36 hours before removing clips.

MICROWAVE METHOD
First check the manufacturer's guide to bottling in your microwave oven. This recipe was tested in an 830 watt microwave oven.

16 small (1.5kg) tomatoes

Peel and halve tomatoes. Pack tomatoes into 2 hot sterilised preserving jars (1 litre/4 cup capacity each), fitted with rubber rings; seal with lids and clips. Cook on medium for 8 minutes, remove jars carefully from oven; cool overnight. Repeat cooking process, remove jars carefully from oven; cool. Stand 36 hours before removing clips.

PRESERVING UNIT
First check the manufacturer's guide to your preserving unit. This recipe was tested in a Fowlers Vacola year rounder food preserver, without a thermostat.

16 small (1.5kg) tomatoes,
**   peeled, halved**
2 tablespoons lemon juice
2 cups (500ml) water
1 tablespoon sugar
1 teaspoon salt

Pack tomatoes into 2 sterilised preserving jars (1 litre/4 cup capacity each), fitted with rubber rings. Add 1 tablespoon juice to each jar. Combine remaining ingredients in medium jug, stir until sugar is dissolved, pour over tomatoes to within 1cm of tops of jars, seal with lids and clips.

Place jars, not touching, into preserving unit, add enough cold water to come 1cm over tops of jars. Process for 1 hour. Remove jars carefully from unit; cool. Stand 36 hours before removing clips.

■ Storage (all methods): In cool, dark place for about 1 year; refrigerate after opening.

LEFT: From back: Sugared Egg Tomatoes; Tomato, Apple and Ginger Fruit Mince. BELOW: Bottled Tomatoes.

Alessi tray from Ventura Design

Slotted spoon from The Bay Tree Kitchen Shop

SPICED TOMATO AND APPLE JAM

2 medium (280g) lemons, halved
4 large (800g) apples, peeled
3 large (750g) tomatoes,
   peeled, chopped
1 cup (250ml) tomato juice
2 teaspoons grated orange rind
1/2 teaspoon ground cinnamon
1/4 teaspoon ground cloves
5 cups (1.1kg) sugar

Squeeze juice from lemons; reserve seeds. You need 1/3 cup (80ml) juice. Remove and reserve cores from apples; chop apples. Tie reserved seeds and cores in piece of muslin.

Combine lemon juice, muslin bag, apples, tomatoes, tomato juice, rind and spices in large pan. Simmer, covered, about 30 minutes or until apples are tender.

Add sugar, stir over heat, without boiling, until sugar is dissolved. Boil, uncovered, stirring occasionally, about 30 minutes or until jam jells when tested on a cold saucer; discard muslin bag. Pour hot jam into hot sterilised jars; seal immediately.

Makes about 1.25 litres (5 cups).

■ Storage: In cool, dark place for about 6 months; refrigerate after opening.

PINEAPPLE, TOMATO AND GINGER JAM

2 medium (280g) lemons
1 large (300g) orange
3 cups (680g) finely chopped
   fresh pineapple
4 large (1kg) tomatoes,
   peeled, chopped
2 tablespoons grated fresh ginger
1/4 teaspoon ground cloves
3 1/2 cups (770g) sugar

Squeeze juice from lemons and orange; reserve seeds. You need 1 cup (250ml) combined juices. Tie reserved seeds in piece of muslin. Combine juices, muslin bag, pineapple, tomatoes, ginger and cloves in large pan. Simmer, covered, about 25 minutes or until tomatoes are pulpy. Add sugar, stir over heat, without boiling, until sugar is dissolved. Boil, uncovered, stirring occasionally, about 30 minutes or until jam jells when tested on a cold saucer; discard muslin bag. Pour hot jam into hot sterilised jars; seal immediately.

Makes about 1 litre (4 cups).

■ Storage: In cool, dark place for about 6 months; refrigerate after opening.

From left: Spiced Tomato and Apple Jam; Pineapple, Tomato and Ginger Jam.

HOT AND SPICY TOMATO PICKLES

2 tablespoons vegetable oil
6 cloves garlic, peeled,
    roughly chopped
2 medium (300g) onions, quartered
2 tablespoons grated fresh ginger
4 small fresh red chillies
1 tablespoon cumin seeds
2 teaspoons garam masala
1 tablespoon ground coriander
10 medium (1.9kg) tomatoes,
    quartered
½ cup (125ml) brown vinegar
1 teaspoon salt
½ cup (100g) firmly packed
    brown sugar
2 tablespoons fish sauce

Blend or process oil, garlic, onions, ginger, chillies and spices until smooth. Combine spice mixture, tomatoes, vinegar, salt and sugar in large pan, stir over heat, without boiling, until sugar is dissolved. Simmer, uncovered, stirring occasionally, 45 minutes.

Add sauce, simmer, uncovered, about 15 minutes or until mixture thickens. Spoon hot pickles into hot sterilised jars; seal immediately.

Makes about 1.5 litres (6 cups).

■ Storage: Refrigerated for about 2 months.

GREEN TOMATO RELISH

6 large (1.5kg) green tomatoes,
    chopped
2 medium (300g) onions, chopped
2 cloves garlic, thinly sliced
1 teaspoon grated fresh ginger
1 cup (250ml) cider vinegar
¼ cup (60ml) brown vinegar
1 cup (220g) sugar
2 teaspoons salt
½ teaspoon ground cardamom
¼ teaspoon ground cloves
½ teaspoon ground cinnamon
½ teaspoon ground turmeric

Combine all ingredients in large pan, stir over heat, without boiling, until sugar is dissolved. Simmer, uncovered, stirring occasionally, about 50 minutes or until mixture thickens. Spoon hot relish into hot sterilised jars; seal immediately.

Makes about 1.25 litres (5 cups).

■ Storage: Refrigerated for about 2 months.

From left: Green Tomato Relish (on roll); Hot and Spicy Tomato Pickles.

GREEN TOMATO JAM

1 medium (180g) orange, halved
1 medium (140g) lemon, halved
¼ cup (60ml) water
4 large (1kg) green tomatoes,
  thinly sliced
3 cups (660g) sugar
¼ cup (55g) glace ginger, sliced

Remove seeds from citrus fruit; tie seeds in piece of muslin. Blend or process unpeeled citrus fruit and water until finely chopped.

Combine citrus mixture with tomatoes in large pan, simmer, uncovered, stirring occasionally, about 10 minutes or until tomatoes are pulpy. Add muslin bag and remaining ingredients to pan, stir over heat, without boiling, until sugar is dissolved. Simmer, uncovered, stirring occasionally, about 30 minutes or until jam jells when tested on a cold saucer; discard muslin bag. Pour hot jam into hot sterilised jars; seal immediately.

Makes about 1.25 litres (5 cups).

■ Storage: In cool, dark place for about 6 months; refrigerate after opening.

TOMATO, LEMON AND PORT MARMALADE

5 medium (700g) lemons
3½ cups (875ml) water
4 cups (880g) sugar, approximately
6 large (1.5kg) tomatoes,
  peeled, chopped
1 cup (220g) sugar, extra
½ cup (125ml) port

Cut unpeeled lemons into 5mm slices. Remove seeds, tie seeds in piece of muslin. Place lemon slices, muslin bag and water in large bowl, cover; stand overnight.

Transfer lemon mixture to large pan, simmer, covered, about 1 hour or until rind is soft, stirring occasionally; discard muslin bag. Measure fruit mixture, allow 1 cup (220g) sugar to each cup of fruit mixture. Return fruit mixture and sugar to pan with tomatoes and extra sugar. Stir over heat, without boiling, until sugar is dissolved. Boil, uncovered, stirring occasionally, about 40 minutes or until mixture is reduced by half. Stir in port, boil, uncovered, about 5 minutes or until marmalade jells when tested on a cold saucer. Pour hot marmalade into hot sterilised jars; seal immediately.

Makes about 1.5 litres (6 cups).

■ Storage: In cool, dark place for about 6 months; refrigerate after opening.

China with words from Home & Garden on the Mall

Soups & Snacks

The tasty and versatile tomato offers unlimited possibilities and adds a great flavour bonus to these delicious soups and snacks. Many of the mouth-watering recipes on these pages can also double as light lunches or starters, too.

TOMATO TAHINI DIP WITH ASPARAGUS

3 small (390g) tomatoes, roughly chopped
1/3 cup (80ml) tahini
1 1/2 tablespoons lemon juice
1 small clove garlic, crushed
1 1/4 cups (310ml) plain yogurt
1 1/2 teaspoons sugar
1/2 teaspoon cracked black peppercorns
2 bunches (500g) asparagus

Blend or process tomatoes until smooth, press through fine sieve; discard pulp. Place tahini in medium bowl, gradually whisk in tomato puree. Whisk in combined juice, garlic, yogurt, sugar and pepper. Cover, refrigerate 1 hour.

Snap off and discard tough ends of asparagus. Add asparagus to large pan of boiling water, drain immediately, rinse under cold water; drain. Serve dip with asparagus.

Makes about 2 1/2 cups (625ml).
■ Dip can be made 2 days ahead.
■ Storage: Covered, in refrigerator.
■ Freeze: Not suitable.
■ Microwave: Asparagus suitable.

MUSHROOM AND TOMATO BRUSCHETTA

28cm bread stick
1/4 cup (60ml) olive oil
300g button mushrooms
30g butter
3 cloves garlic, crushed
1 tablespoon balsamic vinegar
1 tablespoon lemon juice
1 tablespoon drained capers, chopped
1/2 cup (60g) seeded black olives, sliced
2 medium (380g) tomatoes, peeled, seeded, chopped
1/3 cup chopped fresh basil

Trim ends from bread stick, cut bread diagonally into 1cm slices. Brush 1 side of slices with oil; grill or toast on both sides until lightly browned. Remove mushroom stems, slice caps thinly.

Melt butter in large pan, add garlic and mushrooms, cook, stirring, 5 minutes. Add vinegar, juice and capers, cook, stirring, until almost all liquid has evaporated. Transfer mixture to medium bowl; cool. Stir in olives, tomatoes and basil. Spoon onto toasts just before serving.

Makes about 20.
■ Can be made a day ahead.
■ Storage: Toasts, in airtight container. Topping, covered, in refrigerator.
■ Freeze: Not suitable.
■ Microwave: Not suitable.

SUN-DRIED TOMATO BAKED RICOTTA

5 cups (1kg) ricotta cheese
1 cup (150g) drained, finely chopped sun-dried tomatoes in oil
4 eggs, lightly beaten
1 tablespoon chopped fresh oregano leaves
2 cloves garlic, crushed
1/2 cup (60g) seeded black olives, sliced

Grease 2 x 8cm x 26cm bar cake pans, line bases and sides with baking paper.

Combine cheese, tomatoes, eggs, oregano and garlic in large bowl; mix well. Spoon quarter of the mixture into each pan, sprinkle with olives; spread with remaining mixture. Cover pans with foil. Place pans in baking dish with enough boiling water to come halfway up sides of pans. Bake in moderate oven about 1 hour or until firm. Remove foil, bake about 10 minutes or until lightly browned; cool. Cover, refrigerate 3 hours.

Makes 2.
■ Can be made a day ahead.
■ Storage: Covered, in refrigerator.
■ Freeze: Not suitable.
■ Microwave: Not suitable.

Clockwise from back left: Tomato Dip with Asparagus; Mushroom and Tomato Bruschetta; Sun-Dried Tomato Baked Ricotta.

CHILLI TOMATO SOUP

1 tablespoon vegetable oil
8 bacon rashers, chopped
2 medium (300g) onions, chopped
1 medium (350g) leek, chopped
2 cloves garlic, crushed
3 small fresh red chillies, chopped
³/4 cup (180ml) tomato paste
3 large (750g) tomatoes, chopped
1 medium (200g) red pepper,
  chopped
2 litres (8 cups) water
440g can corn kernels,
  rinsed, drained
½ cup firmly packed fresh
  coriander leaves, chopped

TORTILLA CRISPS
26cm tortilla
vegetable oil for shallow-frying

Heat oil in large pan, add bacon, cook, stirring, until browned and crisp; drain on absorbent paper. Add onions, leek, garlic and chillies to same pan, cook, stirring, until onions are soft. Add paste, cook, stirring, 1 minute. Add tomatoes and pepper, simmer, stirring, 5 minutes. Add water, simmer, covered, 30 minutes, remove lid, simmer, uncovered, about 30 minutes or until slightly thickened. Blend or process soup in batches until smooth. Return soup to pan, add bacon, corn and coriander, stir until hot. Serve soup with tortilla crisps.

Tortilla Crisps: Cut tortilla in half, cut each half into 12 wedges. Shallow-fry wedges in batches in hot oil until lightly browned; drain on absorbent paper.

Serves 6.
- Can be made a day ahead.
- Storage: Soup, covered, in refrigerator. Tortilla crisps, in airtight container.
- Freeze: Not suitable.
- Microwave: Soup suitable.

TOMATO, EGGPLANT AND COCONUT SOUP

3 small (690g) eggplants
coarse cooking salt
80g ghee
2 medium (300g) onions, chopped
2 teaspoons grated fresh ginger
2 cloves garlic, crushed
1 small fresh red chilli, chopped
3 teaspoons cumin seeds
2 teaspoons black mustard seeds
1 teaspoon ground coriander
12 fresh curry leaves, torn
6 large (1.5kg) tomatoes, chopped
2 large (600g) potatoes, chopped
2 cups (500ml) vegetable stock
1 cup (250ml) coconut milk
2 tablespoons chopped fresh
  coriander leaves

Cut eggplants into 1cm slices, place in strainer, sprinkle with salt, stand 30 minutes. Rinse eggplant slices under cold water; drain on absorbent paper. Chop eggplant slices.

Melt half the ghee in large pan, add eggplants, cook, stirring, about 10 minutes or until very soft and lightly browned; drain on absorbent paper.

Melt remaining ghee in same pan, add onions, ginger, garlic, chilli, seeds, ground coriander and curry leaves, cook, stirring, until onions are soft. Add tomatoes, potatoes and stock, simmer, covered, about 30 minutes or until potatoes are tender. Remove and reserve curry leaves.

Blend or process tomato mixture in batches until smooth. Press tomato mixture through fine sieve; discard pulp. Return tomato mixture and curry leaves to pan with coconut milk, coriander leaves and eggplants, stir until hot.

Serves 6 to 8.
- Can be made a day ahead.
- Storage: Covered, in refrigerator.
- Freeze: Not suitable.
- Microwave: Not suitable.

CORN AND CHORIZO SAUSAGE MUFFINS

1 cup (150g) self-raising flour
1¹/3 cups (225g) polenta
2 tablespoons caster sugar
3 teaspoons ground cumin
³/4 cup (110g) drained, chopped
  sun-dried tomatoes in oil
1 (180g) chorizo sausage, chopped
130g can creamed corn
1 cup (250ml) buttermilk
3 eggs, lightly beaten
60g butter, melted
¹/3 cup chopped fresh chives

Grease 12 hole (¹/3 cup/80ml capacity) muffin pan. Sift flour into large bowl, add remaining ingredients, stir to combine; do not over-mix. Spoon mixture into prepared pan. Bake in moderately hot oven about 25 minutes.

Makes 12.
- Can be made a day ahead.
- Storage: Airtight container.
- Freeze: Suitable.
- Microwave: Not suitable.

Metal tray from Morris Home & Garden Wares

LEFT: From left: Tomato, Eggplant and Coconut Soup; Chilli Tomato Soup.

SPICY TOMATO PARATHAS

1½ cups (225g) white plain flour
½ cup (80g) wholemeal plain flour
1 tablespoon vegetable oil
¾ cup (180ml) water, approximately
vegetable oil for shallow-frying

SPICY TOMATO FILLING
1 tablespoon olive oil
1 small (80g) onion, finely chopped
1 clove garlic, crushed
1½ teaspoons ground cumin
1½ teaspoons ground coriander
½ teaspoon ground turmeric
4 medium (760g) tomatoes,
    peeled, chopped
2 tablespoons tomato paste

Sift flours into large bowl, stir in oil and enough water to mix to a soft dough. Knead dough on floured surface about 10 minutes or until smooth and elastic. Divide dough into 16 pieces, roll each piece into 16cm round; cover with plastic wrap to prevent drying out.

Spread spicy tomato filling over 8 rounds, leaving 5mm borders. Brush borders with water, top with remaining rounds; press edges together to seal. Shallow-fry parathas, 1 at a time, in hot oil until browned on both sides; drain on absorbent paper.

Spicy Tomato Filling: Heat oil in pan, add onion, garlic and spices, cook, stirring, until onion is soft. Add tomatoes

and paste, simmer, uncovered, stirring occasionally, about 25 minutes or until mixture is thick.

Makes 8.

■ Parathas best made just before serving. Spicy tomato filling can be made a day ahead.
■ Storage: Covered, in refrigerator.
■ Freeze: Not suitable.
■ Microwave: Not suitable.

ABOVE: From left: Spicy Tomato Parathas; Corn and Chorizo Sausage Muffins.

PEPPERY LAMB AND CHICK PEA SALAD

2 teaspoons black peppercorns
1 teaspoon coriander seeds
500g lamb fillets
1 tablespoon olive oil
1 large pita pocket bread
8 medium (600g) egg tomatoes
1½ cups firmly packed fresh
    parsley sprigs, roughly chopped
1 large (300g) red Spanish
    onion, chopped
300g can chick peas,
    rinsed, drained

DRESSING
¼ cup (60ml) lemon juice
¼ cup (60ml) olive oil
1 teaspoon ground cumin
1 teaspoon ground coriander
¼ teaspoon cayenne pepper
2 cloves garlic, crushed
2 teaspoons tomato paste

Lightly crush peppercorns and seeds. Lightly coat lamb with peppercorn mixture. Heat oil in large pan, add lamb in batches, cook until browned and cooked as desired. Stand lamb 10 minutes, slice thickly.

Split bread in half, place on wire rack over oven tray. Toast in moderate oven until lightly browned and crisp; cool. Break bread into small pieces.

Cut tomatoes lengthways into quarters. Combine lamb, parsley, tomatoes, onion, chick peas and dressing in large bowl; mix well. Just before serving, sprinkle with pita toast.

Dressing: Combine all ingredients in jar; shake well.

Serves 4 to 6.

■ Pita toast can be made
  a day ahead.
■ Storage: Airtight container.
■ Freeze: Not suitable.
■ Microwave: Not suitable.

CARAMELISED CUMIN TOMATO SALAD

8 medium (600g) egg tomatoes
1 teaspoon fine sea salt
2 teaspoons sugar
1½ teaspoons cumin seeds
½ teaspoon cracked black
    peppercorns
2 cloves garlic, thinly sliced
¼ cup (60ml) olive oil
1 medium (200g) red pepper
1 small cos lettuce
1 bunch (120g) rocket
½ cup (80g) seeded black olives
½ cup (40g) shaved fresh
    parmesan cheese

DRESSING
¼ cup (60ml) olive oil
2 tablespoons balsamic vinegar
2 teaspoons Dijon mustard

Cut tomatoes in half lengthways. Place tomatoes, cut side up, in deep-sided heavy baking dish, sprinkle with combined salt, sugar, seeds, black pepper and garlic. Bake, uncovered, in very hot oven about 50 minutes or until tomatoes are soft. Drizzle tomatoes with oil, bake 15 minutes; cool.

Quarter red pepper, remove seeds and membranes. Grill pepper, skin side up, until skin blisters and blackens. Peel away skin, thinly slice pepper. Combine torn lettuce leaves, rocket, olives, cheese, tomatoes and red pepper in large bowl, drizzle with dressing.

Dressing: Combine all ingredients in jar; shake well.

Serves 4 to 6.

■ Best made just before serving.
■ Freeze: Not suitable.
■ Microwave: Not suitable.

Bowls and small container from Lady Chef; fabric from St James Furnishings

From left: Caramelised Cumin Tomato Salad; Peppery Lamb and Chick Pea Salad.

SPICY TOMATO SURPRISE SOUFFLES

60g butter
1/3 cup (50g) plain flour
1 cup (250ml) milk
1/2 cup (60g) grated tasty
    cheddar cheese
1/4 cup (30g) grated smoked cheese
1/4 cup (20g) grated fresh
    parmesan cheese
4 egg yolks
2 tablespoons chopped
    fresh parsley
5 egg whites

SPICY TOMATOES
1 tablespoon olive oil
1 small (80g) onion, chopped
2 cloves garlic, crushed
4 small (520g) tomatoes,
    peeled, chopped
1 tablespoon tomato paste
1 small fresh red chilli,
    finely chopped
1/2 teaspoon ground hot paprika
1 teaspoon ground cumin
1 tablespoon water

Grease 6 ovenproof dishes (3/4 cup/ 180ml capacity). Spoon spicy tomatoes into prepared dishes. Melt butter in medium pan, stir in flour, stir over heat until bubbling. Remove from heat, gradually stir in milk, stir over heat until mixture boils and thickens. Remove from heat, stir in cheeses; stir until cheeses are melted. Transfer mixture to large bowl, cool 5 minutes; stir in egg yolks and parsley.

Beat egg whites in medium bowl with electric mixer until firm peaks form. Gently fold egg whites into cheese mixture in 2 batches; spoon into dishes. Place dishes on oven tray. Bake in moderately hot oven about 15 minutes or until souffles are puffed.

Spicy Tomatoes: Heat oil in pan, add onion and garlic, cook, stirring, until onion is soft. Add remaining ingredients, simmer, uncovered, stirring occasionally, about 6 minutes or until mixture is thickened.

Makes 6.

▨ Souffles must be made just before serving. Spicy tomatoes can be made a day ahead.
▨ Storage: Covered, in refrigerator.
▨ Freeze: Not suitable.
▨ Microwave: Not suitable.

THREE-CHEESE AND TOMATO PASTRIES

2 tablespoons olive oil
250g cherry tomatoes
330g yellow teardrop tomatoes
2 cloves garlic, crushed
1 teaspoon sugar
2 1/2 sheets ready-rolled
    puff pastry
1 egg, lightly beaten
1/3 cup (65g) ricotta cheese
1/3 cup (40g) grated gruyere
    cheese
1/2 teaspoon cracked black
    peppercorns

CORIANDER PESTO
3/4 cup firmly packed fresh
    coriander leaves
1/2 cup (40g) coarsely grated
    parmesan cheese
1/2 cup (80g) pine nuts, toasted
2 teaspoons olive oil

Heat oil in pan, add all tomatoes, garlic and sugar, cook, stirring, about 2 minutes or until skins begin to split; drain on absorbent paper.

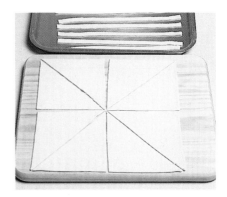

Cut 1 pastry sheet into 1cm strips; cut remaining pastry into 12 triangles. Place triangles about 3cm apart on greased oven trays, brush with some of the egg; prick pastry lightly with fork.

Place strips around edges of triangles; trim to fit, brush strips with more egg. Bake in hot oven about 12 minutes or until lightly browned.

Spread triangles with coriander pesto, top with tomato mixture, then combined cheeses and pepper. Bake in hot oven about 5 minutes or until warm.

Coriander Pesto: Blend or process all ingredients until smooth.

Makes 12.

▨ Pastry triangles and pesto can be made a day ahead.
▨ Storage: Pastry triangles, in airtight container. Pesto, covered, in refrigerator.
▨ Freeze: Not suitable.
▨ Microwave: Not suitable.

ROASTED TOMATO AND BROAD BEAN SOUP

22 large (2kg) egg tomatoes, halved
1 teaspoon salt
1 teaspoon cracked black
    peppercorns
1 tablespoon olive oil
3 small (240g) onions, chopped
3 cloves garlic, crushed
1 tablespoon ground cumin
1 litre (4 cups) vegetable stock
3 1/3 cups (500g) frozen broad beans,
    thawed, peeled
1/4 cup (50g) crumbled feta cheese

CROUTONS
1/2 loaf (400g) unsliced white bread
2 tablespoons olive oil

Place tomatoes, cut side up, on wire racks over baking dishes, sprinkle with salt and pepper. Bake, uncovered, in moderate oven about 1¾ hours or until softened and dehydrated; cool. Heat oil in large pan, add onions, garlic and cumin, cook, stirring, 10 minutes. Add tomatoes and stock, simmer, covered, 15 minutes. Blend or process mixture in batches until smooth. Return mixture to pan, stir in beans; stir until hot. Serve topped with croutons and cheese.

Croutons: Trim crusts from bread, cut bread into 1cm slices. Cut 3.5cm shapes from bread, combine in bowl with oil. Place croutons in single layer on oven trays. Toast in hot oven, turning occasionally, about 15 minutes or until lightly browned and crisp.

Serves 6 to 8.

■ Can be made a day ahead.
■ Storage: Soup, covered, in refrigerator. Croutons in airtight container.
■ Freeze: Not suitable.
■ Microwave: Not suitable.

LEFT: Spicy Tomato Surprise Souffles.
ABOVE: From back: Roasted Tomato and Broad Bean Soup; Three-Cheese and Tomato Pastries.

LAMB BURGERS WITH TOMATO SALSA

1 medium (300g) eggplant
coarse cooking salt
2 tablespoons olive oil
6 bread rolls
1 bunch (120g) rocket
1/2 cup (40g) flaked
    parmesan cheese

PATTIES
600g minced lamb
1 medium (150g) onion,
    finely chopped
2 cloves garlic, crushed
1/3 cup (50g) drained, chopped
    sun-dried tomatoes in oil
1/3 cup (50g) black olives,
    seeded, chopped
3/4 cup (50g) stale breadcrumbs
2 tablespoons finely chopped
    fresh basil
1 egg, lightly beaten

TOMATO SALSA
1 large (350g) red pepper
3 small (390g) tomatoes,
    finely chopped
1 small (100g) red Spanish onion,
    finely chopped
1 teaspoon balsamic vinegar
1 teaspoon finely chopped
    fresh oregano leaves

Cut eggplant into 1.5cm slices, place in strainer, sprinkle with salt, stand 30 minutes. Rinse slices under cold water; drain on absorbent paper. Brush slices with oil, cook in heated griddle pan until browned on both sides and tender. Split rolls, toast lightly. Fill with eggplant, patties, rocket, cheese and tomato salsa.

Patties: Combine all ingredients in medium bowl; mix well. Shape into 6 patties, place on tray, cover, refrigerate 30 minutes. Cook patties in batches in heated greased griddle pan (or grill or barbecue) until browned on both sides and cooked through.

Tomato Salsa: Quarter pepper, remove seeds and membranes. Grill pepper, skin side up, until skin blisters and blackens. Peel away skin, slice pepper thinly. Combine pepper with remaining ingredients in bowl; mix well.

Serves 6.

- ▨ Patties can be prepared
  a day ahead.
- ▨ Storage: Covered, in refrigerator.
- ▨ Freeze: Uncooked patties suitable.
- ▨ Microwave: Not suitable.

CARAMELISED TOMATO AND ONION PIZZA

2 teaspoons (7g) dry yeast
1/2 teaspoon sugar
2/3 cup (160ml) warm water
2 cups (300g) plain flour
1/2 teaspoon salt
2 1/2 tablespoons olive oil
2 cloves garlic, crushed
2 tablespoons tomato paste
1 tablespoon water, extra
1 tablespoon chopped
    fresh oregano leaves
1 1/3 cups (135g) grated
    mozzarella cheese
4 slices (60g) prosciutto, halved
    lengthways
195g jar artichoke hearts in oil,
    drained, quartered

CARAMELISED TOMATOES
6 medium (450g) egg tomatoes,
    halved
1 tablespoon brown sugar
2 teaspoons finely chopped
    fresh rosemary
1/2 teaspoon fine sea salt

CARAMELISED ONIONS
2 tablespoons olive oil
2 large (600g) red Spanish onions,
    finely sliced
2 tablespoons balsamic vinegar
2 tablespoons brown sugar

Combine yeast, sugar and water in small bowl, whisk until yeast is dissolved. Cover, stand in warm place about 10 minutes or until mixture is frothy. Sift flour and salt into large bowl, add yeast mixture and oil, mix to a firm dough. Turn dough onto floured surface, knead about 10 minutes or until dough is smooth and elastic. Place dough in greased bowl, cover, stand in warm place about 1 hour or until doubled in size.

Knead dough on floured surface until smooth, roll to 30cm x 35cm rectangle, place on greased oven tray. Spread combined garlic, paste, extra water and oregano over dough, top with caramelised tomatoes, caramelised onions, cheese, prosciutto and artichokes. Bake in very hot oven about 25 minutes or until browned.

Plate from David Jones; chopping board with drawer from The Pacific East India Company

Fabric from St James Furnishings; copper bowls from The Pacific East India Company

Caramelised Tomatoes: Place tomatoes, cut side up, on wire rack over oven tray, sprinkle with combined remaining ingredients. Bake, uncovered, in moderately hot oven about 45 minutes or until tomatoes are soft.

Caramelised Onions: Heat oil in pan, add onions, cook, stirring occasionally, about 10 minutes or until onions are lightly browned. Add remaining ingredients, stir over low heat about 5 minutes or until onions are soft and mixture is caramelised.

Serves 4 to 6.

■ Best made just before serving.
■ Freeze: Not suitable.
■ Microwave: Not suitable.

LIMA BEAN, TOMATO AND ROCKET SALAD

1³/₄ cups (365g) dried baby white lima beans
9 large (800g) egg tomatoes
1 medium (170g) red Spanish onion, thinly sliced
1 bunch (120g) rocket, roughly chopped
2 tablespoons slivered almonds, toasted

DRESSING
2 cloves garlic, crushed
³/₄ cup (180ml) olive oil
¹/₂ cup (125ml) lemon juice
¹/₄ cup chopped fresh parsley
1¹/₂ tablespoons sugar
3 teaspoons ground sweet paprika
1 teaspoon chilli powder

Place beans in large bowl, cover well with cold water, cover, stand overnight.

Drain beans. Add beans to pan of boiling water, simmer, uncovered, about 35 minutes or until beans are tender. Rinse beans under cold water; drain. Halve tomatoes lengthways, remove seeds, slice tomatoes thinly. Combine beans, tomatoes, onion, rocket and dressing in large bowl; mix well. Serve topped with nuts.

Dressing: Combine all ingredients in jar; shake well.

Serves 6.

■ Can be made 3 hours ahead.
■ Storage: Covered, separately, in refrigerator.
■ Freeze: Not suitable.
■ Microwave: Not suitable.

LEFT: From back: Caramelised Tomato and Onion Pizza; Lamb Burger with Tomato Salsa.
ABOVE: Lima Bean, Tomato and Rocket Salad.

SPINACH CREAM TOMATOES

250g cherry tomatoes
26 leaves (150g) English spinach
1 bacon rasher, finely chopped
185g packaged cream cheese
1 tablespoon lemon juice
1 teaspoon finely chopped
   fresh chives

Trim tops from tomatoes; reserve tops. Scoop out flesh from tomatoes; the flesh is not used in this recipe. Add spinach to pan of boiling water, drain immediately, rinse under cold water; drain. Squeeze excess water from spinach. Add bacon to heated pan, cook, stirring, until browned.

   Process spinach, cheese and juice until smooth; stir in bacon and chives. Spoon cheese mixture into piping bag fitted with plain tube. Pipe spinach cream into tomato shells, add reserved tops.

Makes about 20.

■ Can be prepared 3 hours ahead.
■ Storage: Covered, in refrigerator.
■ Freeze: Not suitable.
■ Microwave: Not suitable.

SUN-DRIED TOMATO AND HERB DIP

2 medium (400g) red peppers
2 x 250g packets cream
   cheese, chopped
2/3 cup (100g) drained, chopped
   sun-dried tomatoes in oil
1/4 cup (30g) seeded black olives,
   roughly chopped
1½ tablespoons chopped
   fresh thyme

Quarter peppers, remove seeds and membranes. Grill peppers, skin side up, until skin blisters and blackens. Peel away skin; chop peppers. Process peppers and remaining ingredients until almost smooth.

Makes about 3½ cups (875ml).

■ Can be made 2 days ahead.
■ Storage: Covered, in refrigerator.
■ Freeze: Not suitable.
■ Microwave: Not suitable.

CRISP POLENTA WITH HALOUMI TOMATO SALSA

3 cups (750ml) water
1½ cups (250g) polenta
1 tablespoon tomato paste
⅓ cup (25g) grated fresh
   parmesan cheese
vegetable oil for shallow-frying

HALOUMI TOMATO SALSA
1 small (100g) red Spanish onion,
   finely chopped
2 medium (380g) tomatoes,
   seeded, finely chopped
¼ cup (35g) drained, chopped
   sun-dried tomatoes in oil
100g haloumi cheese,
   finely chopped
1 small fresh red chilli, chopped
2 tablespoons seeded, chopped
   black olives
1 tablespoon shredded fresh mint
2 teaspoons balsamic vinegar
¼ cup (60ml) lemon juice
¼ cup (60ml) olive oil

Grease 19cm x 29cm rectangular slice pan, line base and sides with plastic wrap. Bring water to boil in medium pan, gradually add polenta, simmer, stirring, about 5 minutes or until mixture is soft and thick. Stir in paste and cheese. Press polenta firmly into prepared pan, cool. Cover, refrigerate 2 hours or until firm.

Turn polenta onto board, trim edges, cut into 12 rectangles. Heat oil in pan, add polenta in batches, shallow-fry until lightly browned on both sides and warmed through. Serve with haloumi tomato salsa.

Haloumi Tomato Salsa: Combine all ingredients in medium bowl; mix well.

Serves 4 to 6.

■ Polenta can be prepared a
   day ahead.
■ Storage: Covered, in refrigerator.
■ Freeze: Not suitable.
■ Microwave: Not suitable.

MINESTRONE WITH CRUSTY HERB BISCOTTI

2 tablespoons olive oil
1 medium (150g) onion, chopped
2 cloves garlic, crushed
1 small (200g) leek, thinly sliced
2 medium (240g) zucchini, sliced
2 small (140g) carrots, sliced
2 small (240g) potatoes, chopped
2 sticks celery, sliced
100g green beans, halved
2 tablespoons tomato paste
1.75 litres (7 cups) chicken stock
2 x 400g cans tomatoes
310g can butter beans,
   rinsed, drained
1 cup (180g) macaroni pasta

China and spoon from Villeroy & Boch.

CRUSTY HERB BISCOTTI
1 cup (150g) self-raising flour
1 cup (150g) plain flour
2 eggs, lightly beaten
2 egg yolks
½ cup (75g) drained, finely chopped
   sun-dried tomatoes in oil,
¼ cup chopped fresh basil
¼ cup chopped fresh coriander
   leaves
1½ cups (120g) grated romano
   cheese
¼ cup (60ml) water, approximately

Heat oil in large pan, add onion, garlic and leek, cook, stirring, until leek is soft. Add zucchini, carrots, potatoes, celery and green beans, cook, stirring, about 5 minutes or until vegetables are softened slightly.

Combine paste in small bowl with a little of the stock, add to vegetable mixture with remaining stock and undrained crushed tomatoes. Simmer, covered, stirring occasionally, about 45 minutes or until vegetables are tender and mixture slightly thickened. Stir in butter beans and pasta, boil, uncovered, about 15 minutes or until pasta is cooked. Serve with crusty herb biscotti.

Crusty Herb Biscotti: Sift flours into medium bowl, add eggs, egg yolks, tomatoes, herbs and cheese. Stir in enough water to mix to a sticky dough. Divide dough in half, roll each half into a 20cm log. Place logs on lightly greased oven tray. Bake in moderate oven about 30 minutes or until firm; stand 10 minutes on tray. Using a serrated knife, cut logs diagonally into 5mm slices. Place biscotti in single layer on oven trays. Bake in slow oven about 25 minutes or until dry and crisp.

Serves 6 to 8.

■ Can be made a day ahead.
■ Storage: Minestrone, covered,
   in refrigerator. Biscotti, in airtight
   container.
■ Freeze: Minestrone suitable.
■ Microwave: Minestrone suitable.

LEFT: From back: Sun-Dried Tomato and Herb Dip; Spinach Cream Tomatoes.
ABOVE: From left: Minestrone with Crusty Herb Biscotti; Crisp Polenta with Haloumi Tomato Salsa.

CHAR-GRILLED OCTOPUS WITH ROASTED TOMATOES

2kg baby octopus
¼ cup (50g) brown sugar
½ cup (125ml) tomato sauce
¼ cup (60ml) barbecue sauce
¼ cup (60ml) Worcestershire sauce
¼ cup (60ml) brown malt vinegar
¼ cup chopped fresh mint
¼ cup chopped fresh
**   coriander leaves**
2 tablespoons olive oil
400g piece haloumi cheese
2 tablespoons lemon juice
1 teaspoon cracked black
**   peppercorns**

ROASTED TOMATOES
10 large (900g) egg tomatoes
2 tablespoons balsamic vinegar
2 tablespoons brown sugar
2 tablespoons olive oil
2 tablespoons chopped fresh mint
2 x 310g cans chick peas,
**   rinsed, drained**

Discard heads and beaks from octopus; cut octopus in half. Combine octopus, sugar, sauces, vinegar and herbs in large bowl; mix well. Cover, refrigerate 3 hours or overnight.

Heat oil in griddle pan, cook octopus in batches (or barbecue) until just tender. Cut cheese into 6 slices. Heat large pan, place cheese in single layer in pan, add juice and pepper, cook until cheese is browned on both sides. Serve octopus on cheese with roasted tomatoes and sauce.

Roasted Tomatoes: Cut tomatoes lengthways into quarters. Combine tomatoes, vinegar, sugar, oil and mint in large baking dish. Bake, uncovered, in moderate oven about 45 minutes or until tomatoes are soft. Remove tomatoes from dish, cover to keep warm. Add chick peas to pan juices in dish, simmer, uncovered, about 3 minutes or until mixture is thickened slightly.

Serves 6.
- Best made just before serving.
- Freeze: Marinated octopus suitable.
- Microwave: Not suitable.

BOUILLABAISSE WITH TOMATO ROUILLE

1kg boneless white fish fillets
1kg uncooked medium prawns
600g small mussels
1 tablespoon olive oil
2 small (160g) onions,
**   finely chopped**
2 sticks celery, finely chopped
4 cloves garlic, crushed
6 small (780g) tomatoes,
**   peeled, chopped**
¼ cup (60ml) tomato paste
8 saffron threads
2 bay leaves
2 cups (500ml) dry white wine
3 large (900g) potatoes,
**   peeled, chopped**
¼ cup chopped fresh flat-leaf
**   parsley**
28cm bread stick, sliced
1 cup (80g) shaved gruyere cheese

FISH STOCK
1 tablespoon olive oil
1 large (200g) onion, chopped
1 large (180g) carrot, chopped
1 stick celery, chopped
3 cloves garlic, crushed
10 black peppercorns
1kg white fish bones, rinsed
1 cup (250ml) dry white wine
1 litre (4 cups) water

TOMATO ROUILLE
2 egg yolks
3 teaspoons Dijon mustard
4 saffron threads
1 tablespoon lemon juice
1 teaspoon tomato paste
1 small (130g) tomato, peeled,
**   seeded, chopped**
1 cup (250ml) olive oil

Cut fish into 4cm pieces. Shell and devein prawns, leaving tails intact. Scrub mussels, remove beards. Heat oil in large pan, add onions, celery and garlic, cook, stirring, until onions are soft and lightly browned.

Tomato-patterned plate and bowls from Horgar Imports; knife and spoon from Home & Garden on the Mall

Tiles from Country Floors; copper pan from The Bay Tree Kitchen Shop

Add fish stock, tomatoes, paste, saffron, bay leaves, wine and potatoes, simmer, covered, about 20 minutes or until potatoes are tender. Add fish and prawns, simmer, uncovered, 3 minutes. Add mussels, simmer, covered, about 3 minutes or until mussels open and seafood is tender. Stir in parsley. Serve bouillabaisse with tomato rouille, bread slices and cheese.

Fish Stock: Heat oil in large pan, add onion, carrot, celery, garlic and peppercorns, cook, stirring, about 10 minutes or until vegetables are soft and lightly browned. Add remaining ingredients, simmer, uncovered, over low heat

15 minutes. Strain stock through muslin; discard bones and pulp. You will need 1.25 litres (5 cups) of stock.

Tomato Rouille: Blend or process egg yolks, mustard, saffron, juice, paste and tomato until smooth. Add oil gradually in a thin stream while motor is operating, blend until thick.

Serves 6 to 8.

- Best made just before serving. Fish stock can be made a day ahead.
- Storage: Covered, in refrigerator.
- Freeze: Stock suitable for 1 month.
- Microwave: Not suitable.

LEFT: Char-Grilled Octopus with Roasted Tomatoes.
ABOVE: Bouillabaisse with Tomato Rouille.

Hand-painted ceramic ware from Kim Elvy Agencies

GAZPACHO

10 medium (1.9kg) tomatoes, peeled, quartered
4 small (500g) Lebanese cucumbers, seeded, chopped
2 medium (340g) red Spanish onions, chopped
3 cloves garlic, peeled, chopped
1/4 cup (60ml) red wine vinegar
1/4 cup (60ml) olive oil
2 teaspoons sugar
2 tablespoons chopped fresh dill
2 teaspoons Tabasco sauce
1 teaspoon cracked black peppercorns
850ml can tomato juice

CROUTONS
1 loaf (900g) unsliced white bread
60g butter
2 tablespoons olive oil

Blend or process tomatoes, cucumbers, onions, garlic, vinegar, oil, sugar, dill, sauce and pepper until roughly chopped, combine in large bowl with juice. Cover, refrigerate 3 hours or overnight. Serve cold gazpacho topped with croutons.

Croutons: Trim crusts from bread, cut bread into 3cm cubes. Heat half the butter and oil in large pan, add half the bread, cook, stirring, until lightly browned and crisp. Repeat with remaining ingredients.

Serves 6.

■ Recipe can be made a day ahead.
■ Storage: Gazpacho, covered, in refrigerator. Croutons, in airtight container.
■ Freeze: Not suitable.
■ Microwave: Not suitable.

TOMATO BACON FLATBREAD WITH SPICY AVOCADO DIP

4 bacon rashers, finely chopped
1 medium (150g) onion, finely chopped
1/2 cup (75g) drained, finely chopped sun-dried tomatoes in oil
2 cups (300g) plain flour
1 teaspoon sugar
2 tablespoons olive oil
2/3 cup (160ml) water, approximately

SPICY AVOCADO DIP
2 medium (500g) avocados, mashed
1/2 cup (125ml) sour cream
1 teaspoon ground cumin
1 teaspoon ground hot paprika
1 teaspoon Tabasco sauce
2 medium (280g) tomatoes, seeded, finely chopped
2 tablespoons lemon juice

Add bacon and onion to pan, cook, stirring, until onion is soft, stir in tomatoes. Sift flour and sugar into medium bowl, add oil and enough water to mix to a soft dough. Knead dough on lightly floured surface until just smooth; divide into 6 pieces.

Roll pieces of dough to 16cm rounds, sprinkle equally with bacon mixture, roll up tightly.

Shape each roll into a coil, dust with flour; roll to 20cm rounds. Cook flatbread, 1 at a time, in heated heavy-based pan until browned on both sides. Serve with spicy avocado dip.

Spicy Avocado Dip: Combine all ingredients in medium bowl; mix well.

Makes 6.

■ Best made close to serving.
■ Freeze: Not suitable.
■ Microwave: Not suitable.

DELICIOUSLY DIFFERENT CAESAR SALAD

2 bunches (500g) fresh asparagus
6 bacon rashers, chopped
30cm bread stick, sliced
500g cherry tomatoes, halved
330g yellow teardrop tomatoes, halved
1 medium cos lettuce
½ cup firmly packed fresh coriander leaves
½ cup (40g) shaved fresh parmesan cheese

GARLIC DRESSING
3 cloves garlic, crushed
2 egg yolks
2 tablespoons balsamic vinegar
2 tablespoons lemon juice
1 teaspoon hot English mustard
⅓ cup loosely packed fresh coriander leaves
6 drained anchovy fillets in oil
1 cup (250ml) olive oil
1 tablespoon tomato paste
½ cup (40g) grated fresh parmesan cheese

Snap off and discard tough ends of asparagus. Cut asparagus into 6cm pieces. Boil, steam or microwave asparagus until just tender, rinse under cold water; drain well. Cook bacon in a dry pan until crisp. Grill bread slices until lightly browned. Combine asparagus, bacon, tomatoes, torn lettuce leaves, coriander, cheese and garlic dressing in large bowl. Just before serving, add bread slices, toss gently.
Garlic Dressing: Blend or process garlic, egg yolks, vinegar, juice and mustard until combined. Add coriander and anchovies, blend until smooth. Gradually add oil in a thin stream while motor is operating, add paste and cheese, blend until thick.

Serves 6.
◼ Dressing can be made a day ahead.
◼ Storage: Covered, in refrigerator.
◼ Freeze: Not suitable.
◼ Microwave: Asparagus suitable.

NUTTY FETTUCCINE SALAD

We used a tomato and herb flavoured fettuccine in this recipe.

10 medium (750g) egg tomatoes
1 teaspoon salt
2 teaspoons sugar
1 teaspoon cracked black peppercorns
10 slices (150g) prosciutto, chopped
375g packet fettuccine pasta
2 bunches (240g) rocket, shredded
½ cup (80g) pine nuts, toasted

DRESSING
½ cup (125ml) olive oil
¼ cup (60ml) red wine vinegar
2 tablespoons chopped fresh basil
1 clove garlic, crushed
¼ cup (20g) grated fresh parmesan cheese
1 teaspoon sugar

Quarter tomatoes lengthways. Place tomatoes, cut side up, on wire racks over oven trays, sprinkle with combined salt, sugar and pepper. Bake, uncovered, in moderate oven about 50 minutes or until browned and soft.

Add prosciutto to hot pan, cook, stirring, until crisp; drain on absorbent paper. Add fettuccine to large pan of boiling water, boil, uncovered, until just tender, drain, rinse under cold water; drain. Combine rocket, nuts, tomatoes, prosciutto and fettuccine in large bowl, add dressing, toss gently.
Dressing: Blend or process all ingredients until smooth.

Serves 6.
◼ Dressing can be made a day ahead.
◼ Storage: Covered, in refrigerator.
◼ Freeze: Not suitable.
◼ Microwave: Pasta suitable.

LEFT: From left: Gazpacho; Tomato Bacon Flatbread with Spicy Avocado Dip.
RIGHT: From back: Deliciously Different Caesar Salad; Nutty Fettuccine Salad.

White bowl from David Jones; large green bowl and jug from The Pacific East India Company

TOMATO, HALOUMI AND SALAMI PIZZAS

2 teaspoons (7g) dry yeast
2 teaspoons sugar
2¼ cups (335g) plain flour
¾ cup (180ml) warm water
2 teaspoons salt
2 tablespoons olive oil
150g sliced hot salami, chopped
225g haloumi cheese, sliced
250g cherry tomatoes, halved
⅓ cup (50g) pine nuts
¼ cup torn fresh large basil leaves

SPICY PASTE

¼ cup (30g) drained sun-dried tomatoes in oil
1 tablespoon tomato paste
¼ cup (40g) seeded black olives
2 cloves garlic, crushed
1 tablespoon olive oil
2 tablespoons shredded fresh basil

Combine yeast, sugar, ¼ cup (35g) of the flour and water in small bowl; whisk until smooth. Cover, stand in warm place about 20 minutes or until mixture is frothy.

Sift remaining flour and salt into large bowl, stir in yeast mixture and oil. Turn dough onto floured surface, knead about 10 minutes or until dough is smooth and elastic. Place dough into greased bowl, cover, stand in warm place about 30 minutes or until dough has almost doubled in size.

Knead dough on floured surface until smooth, divide into 4 pieces. Roll each piece to 20cm round, place rounds on greased oven trays. Spread rounds with spicy paste, leaving 1cm borders, top with salami, cheese, tomatoes and nuts. Bake in moderately hot oven 10 minutes, reduce heat to moderate, bake about 15 minutes or until pizzas are lightly browned; top with basil.

Spicy Paste: Blend or process all ingredients until smooth.

Makes 4.

■ Best made just before serving.
■ Freeze: Not suitable.
■ Microwave: Not suitable.

TOMATO, CHICK PEA AND SPICY SAUSAGE SOUP

8 (800g) fresh spicy Italian sausages
1 tablespoon olive oil
1 stick celery, thinly sliced
1 medium (120g) carrot, finely chopped
1 medium (350g) leek, sliced
2 x 300g cans chick peas, rinsed, drained
1 tablespoon Madras curry paste
8 large (2kg) tomatoes, peeled, chopped
2 teaspoons sugar
¼ cup shredded fresh basil leaves

STOCK

2 tablespoons olive oil
2kg beef bones
4 litres (16 cups) water
1 medium (120g) carrot, roughly chopped
2 sticks celery, roughly chopped
2 bay leaves

Cook sausages in medium pan until browned all over and cooked through, cool 5 minutes. Slice sausages thickly.

Heat oil in large pan, add celery, carrot, leek, chick peas and paste, cook, stirring, until fragrant. Add stock and tomatoes, simmer, uncovered, about 40 minutes or until vegetables are soft. Stir in sausages and sugar; sprinkle with basil.

Stock: Heat oil in large pan, add bones, cook until browned all over. Add remaining ingredients, simmer, uncovered, 1 hour. Strain stock, discard bones and vegetables. You will need about 1.5 litres (6 cups) stock.

Serves 6.

■ Can be made a day ahead.
■ Storage: Covered, in refrigerator.
■ Freeze: Stock suitable.
■ Microwave: Not suitable.

Plate and wooden chopping board from The Pacific East India Company; fabric from St James Furnishings

From left: Tomato, Haloumi and Salami Pizzas; Tomato, Chick Pea and Spicy Sausage Soup.

POTATO WEDGES WITH TOMATO CHILLI SALSA

5 large (1.5kg) potatoes, halved
2 tablespoons olive oil
1 teaspoon fine sea salt
1 teaspoon cracked black
**   peppercorns**
1 teaspoon dried oregano leaves

TOMATO CHILLI SALSA
4 medium (760g) tomatoes,
**   peeled, finely chopped**
1 small (100g) red Spanish onion,
**   finely chopped**
1 small fresh red chilli,
**   finely chopped**
1 tablespoon lime juice
1 tablespoon chopped fresh basil

Cut each potato half into 4 wedges, brush with oil. Place wedges, skin side down, in baking dish. Sprinkle with salt, pepper and oregano. Bake, uncovered, in moderately hot oven about 1 hour or until browned and crisp. Serve with tomato chilli salsa and sour cream, if desired.

Tomato Chilli Salsa: Combine all ingredients in medium bowl; mix well.

Serves 4 to 6.

■ Best made just before serving.
■ Freeze: Not suitable.
■ Microwave: Not suitable.

DELUXE PIZZA BURGERS

6 bread rolls
125g butter, softened
200g tasty cheddar cheese, sliced
2 large (500g) tomatoes, sliced
6 green oak leaf lettuce leaves

PATTIES
¼ cup (60ml) olive oil
1 medium (150g) onion, chopped
2 cloves garlic, crushed
1kg minced beef
1 cup (70g) stale breadcrumbs
¼ cup chopped fresh basil
¼ cup (30g) seeded black olives,
**   chopped**
⅓ cup (25g) coarsely grated fresh
**   parmesan cheese**
1 egg, lightly beaten

CARAMELISED ONIONS
1 tablespoon olive oil
3 large (600g) onions, sliced
2 tablespoons balsamic vinegar
¼ cup (50g) brown sugar

TOMATO SAUCE
4 medium (760g) tomatoes,
**   peeled, chopped**
1 medium (150g) onion, chopped
2 cloves garlic, crushed
1 tablespoon red wine vinegar
1 teaspoon sugar

Split rolls, toast lightly, spread with butter. Top half of each roll with cheese, grill until melted. Fill rolls with patties, tomatoes, lettuce and caramelised onions; top with tomato sauce.

Patties: Heat 1 tablespoon of the oil in pan, add onion and garlic, cook, stirring, until onion is soft. Combine onion mixture with beef in large bowl, then add breadcrumbs, basil, olives, cheese and egg; mix well. Shape mixture into 6 patties. Heat remaining oil in same pan, cook patties in batches until browned on both sides and cooked through. Remove patties, cover to keep warm.

Caramelised Onions: Heat oil in medium pan, add onions and vinegar, cook, stirring, until onions are soft. Add sugar, cook, stirring, until sugar is dissolved; continue to cook, covered, about 15 minutes or until onions are golden brown.

Tomato Sauce: Combine all ingredients in pan, simmer, uncovered, about 15 minutes or until thickened.

Makes 6.

■ Sauce can be made a day
    ahead. Patties can be prepared
    a day ahead.
■ Storage: Covered, separately,
    in refrigerator.
■ Freeze: Uncooked patties suitable.
■ Microwave: Not suitable.

THAI-STYLE PRAWN, MANGO AND TOMATO SALAD

1kg cooked large prawns
3 large (1.8kg) mangoes, chopped
1 large (300g) red Spanish
onion, sliced
1/3 cup firmly packed fresh
coriander leaves
500g cherry tomatoes, halved
660g yellow teardrop tomatoes,
halved
2 tablespoons sesame seeds,
toasted
2 large (640g) avocados, sliced

DRESSING
1 clove garlic, chopped
1 small fresh red chilli
1 medium (190g) tomato,
peeled, quartered
1/2 teaspoon sesame oil
1 1/2 tablespoons lime juice
1 teaspoon sugar
2 teaspoons rice vinegar
2 teaspoons chopped fresh
coriander leaves
1/4 cup (60ml) peanut oil
1 teaspoon grated fresh ginger

Shell and devein prawns, leaving tails intact. Combine prawns with remaining ingredients in large bowl, add dressing, toss gently. Serve on watercress, if desired.

Dressing: Blend or process all ingredients until smooth.

Serves 6.

■ Best made just before serving.
■ Freeze: Not suitable.

LEFT: From back: Deluxe Pizza Burgers; Potato Wedges with Tomato Chilli Salsa.
ABOVE: Thai-Style Prawn, Mango and Tomato Salad.

LAYERED ITALIAN COTTAGE LOAF

23cm round cottage bread loaf
2 large (700g) red peppers
2 large (1kg) eggplants
coarse cooking salt
2 medium (800g) kumara
3 medium (360g) zucchini
½ cup (125ml) olive oil
⅓ cup firmly packed fresh basil
¾ cup (150g) ricotta cheese
¼ cup (20g) grated fresh parmesan cheese

SUN-DRIED TOMATO PASTE
1 cup (150g) drained sun-dried tomatoes in oil
2 cloves garlic, crushed
¼ cup lightly packed fresh oregano leaves
1 tablespoon seeded mustard
¼ cup (60ml) olive oil

Cut 15cm lid from top of loaf, remove soft bread inside loaf, leaving 1.5cm shell. Brush inside lid and bread shell with sun-dried tomato paste. Quarter peppers, remove seeds and membranes. Grill peppers, skin side up, until skin blisters and blackens; peel away skin.

Cut eggplants into 1.5cm slices, place on wire racks over trays, sprinkle with salt; stand 30 minutes. Rinse under cold water; drain on absorbent paper. Cut kumara and zucchini into 5mm slices. Brush all slices with oil, grill until lightly browned; drain on absorbent paper.

Place kumara in bread shell, top with basil, peppers, zucchini, combined cheeses and eggplants; replace lid. Wrap loaf in plastic wrap, place on oven tray, top with another tray, weight with a brick; refrigerate overnight.

Remove plastic wrap. Bake loaf, just before serving, in very hot oven about 10 minutes or until crisp.
Sun-Dried Tomato Paste: Blend or process tomatoes, garlic, oregano and mustard until almost smooth. Add oil gradually in a thin stream while motor is operating; blend until combined.

Serves 6 to 8.

■ Recipe must be prepared a day ahead.
■ Storage: Covered, in refrigerator.
■ Freeze: Not suitable.
■ Microwave: Not suitable.

BELOW: Layered Italian Cottage Loaf.

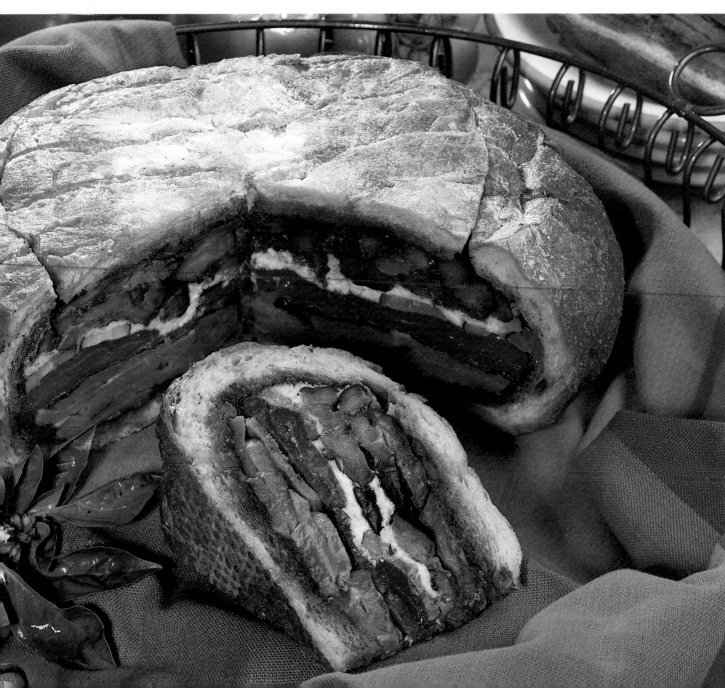

TOMATO BROTH
WITH PRAWNS

24 (1kg) uncooked medium prawns
4 cloves garlic
100g shiitake mushrooms
1 medium (350g) leek
10cm x 24cm sheet fresh lasagne
1 bunch (250g) asparagus
2 teaspoons olive oil
12 medium (2.3kg) tomatoes,
    roughly chopped
5 sprigs fresh parsley
6 black peppercorns
2 bay leaves
2 litres (8 cups) water
100g sugar snap peas
2 medium (380g) tomatoes, seeded,
    finely chopped, extra
2 tablespoons finely shredded
    fresh basil

Shell and devein prawns, leaving tails intact; discard heads, reserve shells. Place unpeeled garlic on oven tray, bake in moderately hot oven about 10 minutes or until garlic is just soft. Remove stems from mushrooms, reserve stems; finely slice caps.

Roughly chop green top of leek, reserve top. Cut remaining leek into thin strips. Cut 1cm x 10cm strips from lasagne sheet. Snap off and discard tough ends of asparagus, chop asparagus. Heat oil in large pan, add prawn shells, cook, stirring, until changed in colour. Squeeze in garlic pulp, add chopped leek and mushroom stems, cook, stirring, about 5 minutes or until leek is soft. Add tomatoes, parsley,

peppercorns, bay leaves and water, simmer, uncovered, 30 minutes, strain; discard pulp.

Return tomato mixture to pan, add prawns, mushroom caps, leek strips, lasagne strips, asparagus and peas, simmer, uncovered, about 5 minutes or until prawns, pasta and vegetables are tender. Just before serving, stir in extra tomatoes and basil.

Serves 6.

■ Best made just before serving.
■ Freeze: Not suitable.
■ Microwave: Not suitable.

MUSHROOM AND
TOMATO RISOTTO

6 slices (90g) prosciutto
4 medium (760g) tomatoes,
    roughly chopped
1 litre (4 cups) chicken stock
30g butter
350g flat mushrooms, sliced
1 tablespoon olive oil
1 large (200g) onion, finely chopped
2 cloves garlic, crushed
2 cups (400g) arborio rice
1/2 cup (125ml) dry white wine
2 tablespoons finely chopped
    fresh parsley
2 teaspoons chopped fresh
    oregano leaves
1/4 cup (20g) grated fresh
    parmesan cheese
1/2 cup (40g) flaked fresh
    parmesan cheese

Grill prosciutto until crisp, cut prosciutto in half. Blend or process tomatoes until smooth, press through fine sieve; discard pulp. Combine tomato liquid with stock in medium pan, bring to boil; cover, keep hot.

Melt butter in large pan, add mushrooms, cook, stirring, until all liquid has evaporated; remove from pan.

Heat oil in same pan, add onion and garlic, cook, stirring, until onion is soft. Add rice; stir to coat with oil. Stir in wine, simmer, uncovered, stirring until wine has been absorbed. Stir in 2/3 cup (160ml) boiling stock mixture, cook, stirring, over low heat until liquid is absorbed.

Continue adding stock mixture gradually, stirring until absorbed before each addition. Total cooking time should be about 35 minutes or until rice is tender. Stir in herbs, grated cheese and mushrooms. Top risotto with prosciutto and flaked cheese.

Serves 4.

■ Best made just before serving.
■ Freeze: Not suitable.
■ Microwave: Not suitable.

*ABOVE: From back: Tomato
Broth with Prawns; Mushroom and
Tomato Risotto.*

ROASTED GARLIC AND YELLOW TOMATO DIP

1 medium (70g) garlic bulb
2 tablespoons olive oil
500g yellow teardrop tomatoes, halved
1 teaspoon sugar
½ teaspoon cracked black peppercorns
250g packet cream cheese
1 tablespoon chopped fresh oregano leaves

PITA TOAST
1 cup (150g) drained sun-dried tomatoes in oil
¼ cup (60ml) olive oil
2 tablespoons chopped fresh parsley
1 tablespoon chopped fresh oregano leaves
4 large pita pocket breads

Brush unpeeled garlic bulb with half the oil; place on oven tray. Bake, uncovered, in moderate oven about 50 minutes or until garlic is soft; cool.

Cut garlic bulb in half, squeeze pulp into bowl. Place tomatoes in baking dish, drizzle with remaining oil, sprinkle with sugar and pepper. Bake, uncovered, in moderate oven about 50 minutes or until tomatoes are very soft; cool.

Blend or process garlic pulp and tomatoes until smooth; press through fine sieve, discard skin and seeds.

Beat cheese in small bowl with electric mixer until light and fluffy, stir in tomato mixture and oregano. Cover, refrigerate 3 hours or overnight. Serve dip with pita toast.

Pita Toast: Blend or process tomatoes, oil and herbs until smooth. Split pita bread in half; spread split side with tomato mixture. Cut each round into 12 wedges. Place wedges, tomato side up, on oven trays, toast in moderate oven about 8 minutes or until crisp.

Makes about 2 cups (500ml).
- Can be made a day ahead.
- Storage: Dip, covered, in refrigerator. Pita toast, in airtight container.
- Freeze: Not suitable.
- Microwave: Not suitable.

OYSTERS GAZPACHO

2 teaspoons olive oil
1 medium (150g) onion, finely chopped
2 cloves garlic, crushed
3 bacon rashers, finely chopped
1 teaspoon ground cumin
2 tablespoons lime juice
1 tablespoon Worcestershire sauce
2 teaspoons Tabasco sauce
1½ cups (375ml) tomato juice
24 fresh oysters in shells
1 teaspoon chopped fresh coriander leaves

Heat oil in pan, add onion, garlic, bacon and cumin, cook, stirring, until onion is soft. Add lime juice and sauces, simmer, uncovered, until almost all liquid has evaporated. Stir in tomato juice, simmer, uncovered, about 15 minutes or until sauce has thickened. Spoon sauce over oysters, grill until lightly browned and heated through. Sprinkle oysters with coriander; serve warm.

Makes 24.
- Can be prepared 3 hours ahead.
- Storage: Covered, in refrigerator.
- Freeze: Not suitable.
- Microwave: Not suitable.

Hand-painted ceramics from Kim Elvy Agencies

RIGHT: From back: Roasted Garlic and Yellow Tomato Dip; Oysters Gazpacho.

Main Courses

Tomatoes add a distinctive flavour to any dish. Whether used as a fruit or vegetable, succulent tomatoes are ideal for salads, in casseroles, for grilling and baking, and are the essential ingredient in many delectable sauces.

LAMB CUTLETS WITH TOMATO TZATZIKI

12 (780g) lamb cutlets
¼ cup (60ml) dry red wine
2 tablespoons olive oil
1 teaspoon crushed dried chillies
½ teaspoon cracked black peppercorns
1 clove garlic, crushed

TOMATO TZATZIKI
2 medium (380g) tomatoes, peeled, finely chopped
2 cloves garlic, crushed
1 small (130g) Lebanese cucumber, seeded, grated
1 tablespoon olive oil
2 cups (500ml) plain yogurt
1 tablespoon lemon juice

Combine lamb, wine, oil, chillies, pepper and garlic in large bowl; mix well. Cover, refrigerate 3 hours or overnight.

Drain lamb from marinade. Cook lamb in batches in heated greased griddle pan (or grill or barbecue) until browned and cooked as desired. Serve with tomato tzatziki.

Tomato Tzatziki: Combine all ingredients in small bowl; mix well.

Serves 4.

- ■ Tomato tzatziki can be made 3 hours ahead.
- ■ Storage: Covered, in refrigerator.
- ■ Freeze: Not suitable.
- ■ Microwave: Not suitable.

ROAST CHICKEN WITH RICE 'N' BACON SEASONING

You will need to cook about 3/4 cup (150g) brown rice for this recipe.

2 teaspoons olive oil
½ medium (85g) red Spanish onion, finely chopped
1 clove garlic, crushed
1 bacon rasher, finely chopped
½ small (100g) red pepper, finely chopped
1½ cups cooked brown rice
¼ cup (35g) corn kernels
2 medium (380g) tomatoes, chopped
2 tablespoons chopped fresh parsley
2kg chicken
2 tablespoons tomato chutney
1 tablespoon tomato paste
1 tablespoon honey

TOMATO CHUTNEY SAUCE
1 cup (250ml) tomato chutney
1 cup (250ml) water
2 medium (380g) tomatoes, peeled, seeded, chopped
½ cup (125ml) dry white wine
2 tablespoons tomato paste

Heat oil in medium pan, add onion, garlic, bacon and pepper, cook, stirring, until onion is soft. Remove from heat, stir in rice, corn, tomatoes and parsley. Fill chicken with rice mixture, secure openings with toothpicks. Tie legs together, tuck wings under. Place chicken in baking dish. Bake, uncovered, in moderately hot oven 1 hour. Brush chicken with combined chutney, paste and honey. Bake, uncovered, about 30 minutes or until chicken is tender. Serve with tomato chutney sauce.

Tomato Chutney Sauce: Combine all ingredients in small pan, simmer, uncovered, about 10 minutes or until thickened; strain.

Serves 6.

- ■ Rice mixture and sauce can be made a day ahead.
- ■ Storage: Covered, in refrigerator.
- ■ Freeze: Not suitable.
- ■ Microwave: Not suitable.

From back: Roast Chicken with Rice 'n' Bacon Seasoning; Lamb Cutlets with Tomato Tzatziki.

MARINATED SPATCHCOCKS WITH TOMATO MAYONNAISE

4 x 500g spatchcocks
1 tablespoon white vinegar
1 tablespoon sugar

MARINADE
400g can tomatoes
4 cloves garlic, peeled, roughly chopped
2 small fresh red chillies, roughly chopped
1 tablespoon grated fresh ginger
1 tablespoon roughly chopped fresh coriander root
1 tablespoon roughly chopped fresh lemon grass
1 tablespoon honey
1 tablespoon light soy sauce

TOMATO MAYONNAISE
2 egg yolks
1 tablespoon white vinegar
1 teaspoon French mustard
1 cup (250ml) olive oil
2 medium (380g) tomatoes, peeled, seeded, finely chopped
2 tablespoons finely chopped fresh coriander leaves

Using poultry shears or scissors, cut along both sides of spatchcocks' backbones, discard backbones. Cut spatchcocks into quarters. Combine spatchcocks with marinade in large bowl, cover, refrigerate 3 hours or overnight.

Drain spatchcocks from marinade; reserve marinade. Place spatchcocks on wire rack over baking dish. Bake, uncovered, in moderate oven about 40 minutes or until spatchcocks are cooked through.

Place reserved marinade, vinegar and sugar in small pan, bring to boil, simmer, uncovered, about 5 minutes or until thickened slightly. Serve spatchcocks with marinade mixture and tomato mayonnaise.

Marinade: Blend or process undrained tomatoes with remaining ingredients until smooth.

Tomato Mayonnaise: Blend or process egg yolks, vinegar and mustard until smooth. Add oil gradually in a thin stream while motor is operating, stir in remaining ingredients.

Serves 4.

■ Spatchcocks can be prepared a day ahead. Tomato mayonnaise can be made a day ahead.
■ Storage: Covered, in refrigerator.
■ Freeze: Not suitable.
■ Microwave: Not suitable.

KANGAROO FILLETS WITH BASIL GARLIC TOMATOES

6 (1kg) kangaroo loin fillets
1 cup (250ml) dry red wine
1 medium (150g) onion, chopped
1 teaspoon cracked black peppercorns
3 cloves garlic, sliced
1/4 cup chopped fresh basil
1/4 cup (60ml) Worcestershire sauce
2 tablespoons balsamic vinegar
2 tablespoons brown sugar

BASIL GARLIC TOMATOES
12 medium (900g) egg tomatoes
4 cloves garlic
24 fresh basil leaves
1/2 teaspoon cracked black peppercorns
2 tablespoons olive oil

Combine kangaroo with remaining ingredients in large bowl, cover; refrigerate 3 hours or overnight.

Remove kangaroo from marinade, reserve marinade. Cook kangaroo in batches in heated greased griddle pan (or grill or barbecue) about 5 to 8 minutes or until cooked as desired. Cover, stand 10 minutes before slicing.

Place reserved marinade in small pan, bring to boil, simmer, uncovered, about 5 minutes or until thickened slightly; strain. Serve kangaroo with marinade mixture and basil garlic tomatoes.

Basil Garlic Tomatoes: Halve tomatoes lengthways. Using a skewer, make a small hole in side of each half. Peel garlic, cut garlic lengthways into 24 slices. Push a basil leaf and a slice of garlic into each hole. Place tomatoes, cut side up, in baking dish, sprinkle with pepper, drizzle with oil. Bake, uncovered, in very slow oven about 3 hours or until tomatoes are soft and edges are shrivelled.

Serves 4 to 6.
■ Best made just before serving.
■ Freeze: Marinated kangaroo suitable.
■ Microwave: Not suitable.

LEFT: From back: Marinated Spatchcocks with Tomato Mayonnaise; Kangaroo Fillets with Basil Garlic Tomatoes.

Plates and serviette from The Bay Tree Kitchen Shop; cutlery from Home & Garden on the Mall

TOMATO BASIL RATATOUILLE ON EGGPLANT

1 tablespoon olive oil
1 medium (150g) onion, thinly sliced
2 cloves garlic, crushed
2 bacon rashers, chopped
2 medium (180g) zucchini, chopped
2 medium (400g) red peppers, chopped
1 medium (200g) green pepper, chopped
6 medium (1kg) tomatoes, peeled, seeded, chopped
1/4 cup (60ml) tomato paste
1/2 cup (125ml) dry white wine
1/2 cup (125ml) chicken stock
2 teaspoons sugar
1/4 cup shredded fresh basil
12 (700g) finger eggplants
1/3 cup (80ml) olive oil, extra
1 cup (80g) flaked fresh parmesan cheese

Heat oil in large pan, add onion, garlic and bacon, cook, stirring, until onion is soft. Add zucchini and peppers with tomatoes, paste, wine, stock, sugar and basil, simmer, uncovered, about 15 minutes or until vegetables are soft and mixture has thickened.

Cut eggplants lengthways into 1cm slices, brush with extra oil. Cook eggplant slices in batches in heated griddle pan (or grill or barbecue) until browned and tender. Place eggplant slices on serving plates, top with ratatouille mixture, sprinkle with cheese.

Serves 4.

■ Best made just before serving.
■ Freeze: Not suitable.
■ Microwave: Not suitable.

MARINATED CHICKEN AND TOMATO KEBABS

9 (1kg) chicken thigh fillets
1/4 cup (60ml) lime juice
1/4 cup (60ml) olive oil
1/4 cup chopped fresh garlic chives
1/4 cup chopped fresh mint
2 teaspoons sambal oelek
2 teaspoons sugar
2 teaspoons cracked black peppercorns
500g cherry tomatoes, halved
330g yellow teardrop tomatoes

MINTED LIME SAUCE
1/2 cup (125ml) white wine vinegar
2 green shallots, chopped
2 bay leaves
6 black peppercorns
1/4 cup (60ml) lime juice
4 egg yolks
250g butter, melted
2 medium (380g) tomatoes, seeded, chopped
2 teaspoons grated lime rind
2 tablespoons chopped fresh mint

Plates from Country Floors

Cut chicken into 3cm pieces. Combine chicken, juice, oil, chives, mint, sambal oelek, sugar and pepper in medium bowl; mix well. Cover, refrigerate 3 hours or overnight.

Thread chicken and tomatoes onto 18 skewers. Cook skewers in batches in heated greased griddle pan (or grill or barbecue) until chicken is tender. Serve with minted lime sauce.

Minted Lime Sauce: Combine vinegar, shallots, leaves, peppercorns and juice in small pan, simmer, uncovered, about 5 minutes or until reduced to 2 tablespoons, strain; discard shallot mixture. Whisk vinegar mixture and egg yolks in medium bowl until creamy, gradually whisk in hot butter, whisk until mixture is thick. Stir in tomatoes, rind and mint.

Makes 18.

■ Best made just before serving.
■ Freeze: Not suitable.
■ Microwave: Not suitable.

ABOVE: From back: Tomato Basil Ratatouille on Eggplant; Marinated Chicken and Tomato Kebabs.

CHICKEN WITH CHEESE 'N' BACON FILLING

4 large (1kg) chicken breast fillets
2 teaspoons olive oil
2 cups (500ml) chicken stock
425g can tomatoes
2 tablespoons tomato paste
2 teaspoons cornflour

FILLING
2 teaspoons olive oil
1 medium (150g) onion,
    finely chopped
2 cloves garlic, crushed
4 bacon rashers, finely chopped
½ bunch (250g) English spinach,
    chopped
2 tablespoons drained, chopped
    sun-dried tomatoes in oil
1 tablespoon shredded fresh basil
1 cup (125g) grated tasty
    cheddar cheese
½ cup (100g) ricotta cheese

Place 1 fillet, smooth side down, on board. Make a shallow cut lengthways down centre of fillet, then cut evenly from centre to 1 side to create a flap; repeat on other side. Open out flaps, flatten gently to make even thickness throughout. Repeat with remaining fillets. Place filling lengthways along centres of fillets, fold over edges to enclose filling; secure with toothpicks.

Heat oil in large pan, add chicken, cook until browned all over; remove from pan. Add 1¾ cups (430ml) of the stock, undrained crushed tomatoes and paste to pan, simmer, uncovered, 5 minutes. Stir in blended cornflour and remaining stock, stir over heat until mixture boils and thickens slightly. Return chicken to pan, simmer, covered, about 20 minutes or until cooked through.

Filling: Heat oil in medium pan, add onion, garlic and bacon, cook, stirring, until onion is soft. Add spinach, stir over heat until spinach is wilted; cool 5 minutes. Stir in tomatoes, basil and both cheeses.

Serves 4.

▓ Filling can be made a day ahead.
▓ Storage: Covered, in refrigerator.
▓ Freeze: Not suitable.
▓ Microwave: Not suitable.

MUSTARD LAMB RACKS WITH SUN-DRIED TOMATO CRUST

2 teaspoons olive oil
4 racks of lamb (4 cutlets in each)
1 tablespoon French mustard
1 cup (70g) stale breadcrumbs
2 cloves garlic, crushed
1 tablespoon chopped fresh thyme
¼ cup (35g) drained, finely chopped
    sun-dried tomatoes in oil
1 egg white, lightly beaten

FRESH THYME SAUCE
½ cup (125ml) beef stock
1 tablespoon red wine vinegar
1 cup (250ml) tomato juice
1 teaspoon cornflour
1 tablespoon water
1 tablespoon drained, chopped
    sun-dried tomatoes in oil
1 teaspoon chopped fresh thyme

Heat oil in baking dish, add lamb, cook until browned; cool 5 minutes. Spread mustard over backs of lamb racks. Combine remaining ingredients in small bowl, press over mustard. Return lamb, crust side up, to baking dish. Bake, uncovered, in moderately hot oven about 25 minutes or until cooked as desired. Serve with fresh thyme sauce. Serve with char-grilled vegetables, if desired.

Fresh Thyme Sauce: Combine stock, vinegar and juice in small pan, simmer, uncovered, about 15 minutes or until reduced to about 1 cup (250ml). Stir in blended cornflour and water, stir over heat until sauce boils and thickens slightly; stir in tomatoes and thyme.

Serves 4.

■ Lamb can be prepared 3 hours
    ahead. Sauce can be made
    a day ahead.
■ Storage: Covered, in refrigerator.
■ Freeze: Not suitable.
■ Microwave: Not suitable.

From left: Chicken with Cheese 'n' Bacon Filling; Mustard Lamb Racks with Sun-Dried Tomato Crust.

Yellow and blue plate from Opus Design; wire basket from Accoutrement

TOMATO CHICKEN RISOTTO

1 medium (200g) red pepper
1.5 litres (6 cups) chicken stock
2 cups (500ml) tomato juice
1 cup (250ml) dry white wine
1/4 cup (60ml) olive oil
5 (550g) chicken thigh fillets,
  finely chopped
2 cloves garlic, crushed
200g Swiss brown mushrooms,
  sliced
100g pancetta, chopped
2 cups (400g) arborio rice
1/2 cup (75g) drained, thinly sliced
  sun-dried tomatoes in oil
1 tablespoon chopped fresh sage
2 teaspoons chopped fresh thyme

Quarter pepper, remove seeds and membranes. Grill pepper, skin side up, until skin blisters and blackens. Peel away skin, finely chop pepper. Combine stock, juice and wine in medium pan, bring to boil; cover, keep hot.

Heat half the oil in large pan, add chicken, cook, stirring, until browned; drain on absorbent paper. Heat remaining oil in same pan, add garlic, mushrooms and pancetta, cook, stirring, until pancetta is browned. Add rice; stir to coat with oil. Stir in 1 cup (250ml) boiling stock mixture, cook, stirring, over low heat until liquid is absorbed.

Add chicken to rice mixture, continue adding stock mixture gradually, stirring until absorbed before each addition. Total cooking time should be about 35 minutes or until rice is tender. Stir in tomatoes, herbs and pepper.

Serves 6.

■ Best made just before serving.
■ Freeze: Not suitable.
■ Microwave: Not suitable.

PASTA WITH GARLIC CRUMBS

11 large (1kg) egg tomatoes, halved
1 tablespoon finely chopped
  fresh oregano leaves
1/2 teaspoon salt
1/2 teaspoon cracked black
  peppercorns
1/3 cup (80ml) olive oil
5 cups (350g) stale breadcrumbs
3 cloves garlic, crushed
1 tablespoon lemon juice
1/2 cup (80g) pine nuts
1/2 cup finely shredded fresh basil
1/4 cup finely chopped fresh
  oregano leaves, extra
500g linguine pasta
1 1/4 cups (200g) black olives, seeded
1/4 cup (60ml) olive oil, extra
1/4 cup (20g) flaked fresh
  parmesan cheese

Place tomatoes, cut side up, on wire rack over oven tray; sprinkle with combined oregano, salt and pepper. Bake, uncovered, in hot oven about 45 minutes or until tomatoes are soft.

Heat oil in large pan, add breadcrumbs, garlic and juice, cook, stirring, over low heat about 10 minutes or until crisp. Add nuts, basil and extra oregano, cook, stirring, about 10 minutes or until nuts are lightly browned.

Meanwhile, add pasta to large pan of boiling water, boil, uncovered, until just tender; drain. Just before serving, combine hot pasta with crumb mixture, olives and extra oil; serve over tomatoes and cheese.

Serves 4 to 6.

■ Best made just before serving.
■ Freeze: Not suitable.
■ Microwave: Pasta suitable.

BARBECUED SEAFOOD WITH BROAD BEAN SALAD

1.2kg uncooked large prawns
1kg baby octopus
2 tablespoons olive oil
2 tablespoons tomato paste
4 medium (760g) tomatoes
2 cups (300g) frozen broad beans,
  thawed, peeled
1 bunch (120g) rocket
1/2 cup (100g) crumbled feta cheese

DRESSING
4 medium (300g) egg tomatoes,
  halved
1 clove garlic, bruised
1 sprig fresh oregano
1/2 cup (125ml) olive oil
1 tablespoon sugar

Shell and devein prawns, leaving tails intact. Discard heads and beaks from octopus; cut octopus into quarters. Combine prawns, octopus, oil and paste in large bowl; mix well.

Add seafood to heated greased griddle pan in batches (or grill or barbecue) until lightly browned and tender. Cut tomatoes into thick wedges, combine in bowl with beans, rocket, seafood and dressing; top with cheese.

Dressing: Combine tomatoes, garlic, oregano and 1 tablespoon of the oil in large baking dish; sprinkle with sugar. Bake, uncovered, in moderate oven about 1 hour or until tomatoes are soft; cool. Blend or process tomatoes with pan juices until almost smooth, press through fine sieve, discard pulp. Whisk in remaining oil.

Serves 4.

■ Dressing can be made a day ahead.
■ Storage: Covered, in refrigerator.
■ Freeze: Not suitable.
■ Microwave: Not suitable.

Clockwise from left: Tomato Chicken Risotto; Pasta with Garlic Crumbs; Barbecued Seafood with Broad Bean Salad.

China from Villeroy & Boch

Mesh strainer from Accoutrement; enamel ware from Storehouse

BRAISED LAMB SHANKS WITH CHEESE POLENTA

2 tablespoons olive oil
8 medium (1.5kg) lamb shanks
2 large (600g) red Spanish onions, sliced
3 cloves garlic, crushed
13 medium (2.5kg) fresh tomatoes, peeled, chopped
2 bay leaves
2 cups (500ml) beef stock
½ cup (125ml) dry red wine
⅓ cup (80ml) madeira
¼ cup (60ml) tomato paste
200g small Swiss brown mushrooms
¾ cup (110g) drained, chopped sun-dried tomatoes in oil
2 teaspoons finely chopped fresh rosemary

CHEESE POLENTA
1 litre (4 cups) chicken stock
1 cup (170g) polenta
½ cup (40g) grated romano cheese
¼ cup (30g) grated tasty cheddar cheese
2 tablespoons finely shredded fresh basil
plain flour
vegetable oil for shallow-frying

Heat oil in large pan, add lamb in batches, cook until browned all over. Return lamb to pan with onions and garlic, cook, stirring occasionally, until onions are soft. Add fresh tomatoes, leaves, stock, wine, madeira and paste, simmer, covered, about 1 hour or until tomatoes are pulpy. Stir in remaining ingredients, simmer, uncovered, about 30 minutes or until lamb is tender.

Remove lamb; cover to keep warm. Simmer tomato mixture in pan, uncovered, about 15 minutes or until thickened, serve over lamb. Serve with cheese polenta.

Cheese Polenta: Bring stock to boil in medium pan, gradually add polenta, simmer, stirring, about 15 minutes or until very thick. Remove from heat, stir in cheeses and basil. Press mixture firmly into greased 20cm x 30cm lamington pan; cool. Cover, refrigerate 1 hour or until firm.

Cut polenta in half lengthways, then into 2cm pieces widthways. Coat polenta in flour, shallow-fry in batches in hot oil until lightly browned; drain on absorbent paper.

Serves 4 to 6.

■ Lamb shanks can be braised a day ahead. Cheese polenta can be prepared a day ahead.
■ Storage: Covered, separately, in refrigerator.
■ Freeze: Not suitable.
■ Microwave: Not suitable.

CHICKEN CACCIATORE

2 tablespoons olive oil
12 (1.9kg) chicken thigh cutlets
1 large (200g) onion, sliced
2 cloves garlic, crushed
1 medium (200g) red pepper, sliced
2 x 400g cans tomatoes
½ cup (125ml) chicken stock
½ cup (125ml) dry white wine
¼ cup (60ml) tomato paste
1 sprig fresh rosemary
1 bay leaf
½ cup (80g) seeded black olives

Heat oil in large pan, add chicken in batches, cook until browned all over; drain. Add onion, garlic and pepper to pan, cook, stirring, until onion is soft. Stir in undrained crushed tomatoes, stock, wine, paste, rosemary and bay leaf. Add chicken, simmer, covered, about 30 minutes or until tender. Add olives, simmer, uncovered, about 10 minutes or until sauce thickens; discard rosemary and bay leaf.

Serves 4 to 6.

■ Can be made a day ahead.
■ Storage: Covered, in refrigerator.
■ Freeze: Suitable.
■ Microwave: Not suitable.

ABOVE: From left: Braised Lamb Shanks with Cheese Polenta; Chicken Cacciatore. RIGHT: Blue Cheese and Roasted Tomato Tart.

BLUE CHEESE AND ROASTED TOMATO TART

7 medium (525g) egg tomatoes
¹/₂ teaspoon salt
¹/₂ teaspoon cracked black peppercorns
2 teaspoons olive oil
2 medium (300g) onions, thinly sliced
2 cloves garlic, crushed
100g pancetta, chopped
¹/₃ cup chopped fresh chives
100g blue vein cheese, chopped
4 eggs, lightly beaten
¹/₂ cup (125ml) cream

PASTRY
1¹/₂ cups (225g) plain flour
125g butter, chopped
1 egg yolk
2 tablespoons grated parmesan cheese
1¹/₂ tablespoons cold water, approximately

Halve tomatoes lengthways. Place tomatoes, cut side up, on wire rack over baking dish; sprinkle with salt and pepper. Bake, uncovered, in moderate oven 1 hour; cover, bake about 1¹/₂ hours or until tomatoes are partly dehydrated, but soft inside; cool 15 minutes.

Heat oil in medium pan, add onions, garlic, pancetta and chives, cook, stirring, about 10 minutes or until onions are soft and lightly browned; cool 15 minutes.

Sprinkle cheese over base of pastry case, top with onion mixture then combined eggs and cream. Place tomatoes, cut side up, over filling. Bake in moderate oven about 1 hour or until lightly browned and set; cover with foil if overbrowning. Stand 5 minutes before serving.

Pastry: Grease 21cm x 28.5cm rectangular loose-base flan tin or 28cm round loose-base flan tin. Process flour and butter until combined. Add egg yolk, cheese and enough water to make ingredients cling together. Knead dough on lightly floured surface until smooth, cover, refrigerate 30 minutes.

Roll pastry between sheets of baking paper until large enough to line prepared tin. Press pastry into tin, trim edges, lightly prick base with fork, refrigerate 30 minutes.

Cover pastry with baking paper, fill with dried beans or rice, place on oven tray. Bake in moderately hot oven 10 minutes, remove paper and beans, bake about 10 minutes or until lightly browned; cool.

Serves 6 to 8.

■ Best made just before serving.
■ Freeze: Not suitable.
■ Microwave: Not suitable.

BARBECUED FISH WITH POTATO SALAD

We used blue-eyed cod fillets for this recipe.

10 baby (400g) new potatoes, halved
4 (1kg) firm white fish fillets
1 bunch (250g) asparagus
2 medium (380g) tomatoes, quartered
330g yellow teardrop tomatoes, halved
100g mixed baby salad leaves

CITRUS DRESSING
⅓ cup (80ml) orange juice
2 tablespoons olive oil
2 teaspoons white wine vinegar
1 tablespoon chopped fresh coriander leaves
½ teaspoon cracked black peppercorns

Boil or steam potatoes until tender; drain. Place potatoes, cut side down, in batches in heated greased griddle pan, cook (or grill or barbecue) until browned and crisp. Add fish to heated greased griddle pan, cook (or grill or barbecue) until browned and tender; cool. Remove any bones from fish, roughly chop fish.

Snap off and discard tough ends of asparagus, halve asparagus. Boil, steam or microwave asparagus until just tender, drain, rinse under cold water; drain. Combine potatoes, fish, asparagus, tomatoes and leaves in large bowl, drizzle with citrus dressing.
Citrus Dressing: Combine all ingredients in jar; shake well.

Serves 4.
■ Barbecued fish best cooked just before serving. Citrus dressing can be made a day ahead.
■ Storage: Covered, in refrigerator.
■ Freeze: Not suitable.
■ Microwave: Asparagus suitable.

QUICK 'N' EASY FISH WITH TOMATO MANGO SALSA

12 x 120g firm white fish fillets
5 medium (950g) tomatoes, seeded, chopped
1 large (600g) mango, chopped
1 medium (170g) red Spanish onion, chopped
1 medium (250g) avocado, chopped
1 fresh kaffir lime leaf, finely chopped
1 teaspoon finely chopped lemon grass
1 teaspoon fish sauce
1 tablespoon orange juice
2 tablespoons lime juice
1 tablespoon tomato juice
1 tablespoon peanut oil
1 tablespoon shredded fresh coriander leaves
1 tablespoon shredded fresh mint

Cook fish in batches in heated greased griddle pan (or grill or barbecue) until browned and cooked through. Cover to keep hot. Combine remaining ingredients in medium bowl, serve with fish.

Serves 6.
■ Best made just before serving.
■ Freeze: Not suitable.
■ Microwave: Not suitable.

From back: Quick 'n' Easy Fish with Tomato Mango Salsa; Barbecued Fish with Potato Salad.

PEPPERY TOMATO, LEEK AND ARTICHOKE RAVIOLI

14 slices (200g) prosciutto
2¼ cups (335g) plain flour
¼ cup (60ml) tomato paste
2 eggs, lightly beaten
2 tablespoons water
2 tablespoons olive oil
2 teaspoons cracked black
  peppercorns
1 egg, lightly beaten, extra
125g butter, melted
1 tablespoon shredded fresh basil
1 tablespoon chopped fresh
  oregano leaves
1 tablespoon shredded fresh
  parsley

FILLING
1 tablespoon olive oil
1 small (200g) leek, chopped
2 cloves garlic, crushed
½ x 280g jar artichoke hearts in oil,
  drained, finely chopped
2 tablespoons drained capers,
  chopped
2 medium (380g) tomatoes,
  seeded, chopped
⅓ cup (25g) coarsely grated fresh
  parmesan cheese

Halve prosciutto slices lengthways, then widthways. Thread prosciutto onto toothpicks, grill until crisp, remove from toothpicks.

Process flour, paste, eggs, water, oil and pepper until mixture forms a ball. Knead dough on lightly floured surface until smooth. Divide mixture into 4 pieces, roll each piece through pasta machine set on thickest setting. Fold dough in half, roll through machine; repeat rolling several times, dusting dough with a little extra flour when necessary. Roll dough through machine, adjusting setting so dough becomes thinner with each roll, dust with extra flour when necessary. Roll to third thinnest setting (1mm thick).

Cut 64 x 7cm rounds from dough, re-rolling any scraps. Brush half the rounds with extra egg, top with rounded teaspoons of filling. Top with remaining rounds; press edges together. Add ravioli to large pan of boiling water, boil, uncovered, about 5 minutes or until just tender; drain. Combine ravioli with combined butter and herbs; top with prosciutto.

Filling: Heat oil in pan, add leek and garlic, cook, stirring, until leek is soft. Remove from heat, stir in remaining ingredients.

Serves 4.

■ Best made just before serving.
■ Freeze: Not suitable.
■ Microwave: Filling suitable.

China from Villeroy & Boch; glasses from Sirocco Homewares

TUNA, TOMATO AND CASHEW SALAD

28cm bread stick, sliced
600g piece tuna fillet, halved
    lengthways
1 teaspoon ground black
    peppercorns
1 teaspoon fine sea salt
2 teaspoons olive oil
11 large (1kg) egg tomatoes,
    quartered
500g bocconcini cheese,
    quartered
1 bunch (120g) rocket
1 cup (150g) unsalted roasted
    cashews

DRESSING
1/4 cup firmly packed fresh
    coriander leaves
1/4 cup firmly packed fresh
    basil leaves
2 cloves garlic, crushed
1 tablespoon drained sun-dried
    tomatoes in oil
1 tablespoon tomato paste
1/4 cup (60ml) olive oil
2 tablespoons lemon juice
1 1/2 tablespoons packaged
    ground almonds
1/4 cup (20g) coarsely grated fresh
    parmesan cheese
1/3 cup (80ml) hot water

Grill bread slices until browned on both sides; cool. Sprinkle tuna with combined pepper and salt. Heat oil in medium pan, add tuna, cook about 1 minute on each side or until tuna is browned but still pink inside. Stand 5 minutes before cutting into 1cm slices. Place tomatoes, cheese, rocket, nuts, tuna and bread on plates; top with dressing.

Dressing: Blend or process herbs, garlic, tomatoes and paste until combined. Add oil gradually in a thin stream while motor is operating. Add remaining ingredients, blend until smooth.

Serves 4.

- Dressing can be made a day ahead.
- Storage: Covered, in refrigerator.
- Freeze: Not suitable.
- Microwave: Not suitable.

CRISP GARLIC SARDINES

500g fresh sardine fillets
plain flour
2 eggs, lightly beaten
2 tablespoons milk
2 cloves garlic, crushed
2 cups (140g) stale breadcrumbs
2/3 cup (50g) coarsely grated fresh
    parmesan cheese
1/4 cup chopped fresh parsley
vegetable oil for deep-frying
125g fettuccine pasta
50g butter, melted
1 teaspoon ground black
    peppercorns

TOMATO SAUCE
1 tablespoon olive oil
1 large (200g) onion, finely chopped
1/2 teaspoon ground cloves
1 1/2 teaspoons mild curry powder
2 tablespoons sugar
1 tablespoon white wine vinegar
1 cup (250ml) tomato juice
2 small (260g) tomatoes, seeded,
    chopped

Coat sardines in flour, dip into combined eggs, milk and garlic, then into combined crumbs, cheese and parsley. Deep-fry sardines in batches in hot oil until browned and cooked through; drain on absorbent paper.

Add pasta to large pan of boiling water, boil, uncovered, until just tender; drain. Combine pasta with butter and pepper. Serve sardines with pasta and hot tomato sauce.

Tomato Sauce: Heat oil in small pan, add onion, cook, stirring, until onion is soft. Add spices, cook, stirring, until fragrant. Stir in sugar, vinegar and juice, simmer, uncovered, about 10 minutes or until sauce thickens slightly. Stir in tomatoes, stir until hot.

Serves 4.

- Sardines can be prepared a day ahead. Tomato sauce can be made a day ahead.
- Storage: Covered, separately, in refrigerator.
- Freeze: Not suitable.
- Microwave: Not suitable.

LEFT: From back: Peppery Tomato, Leek and Artichoke Ravioli; Tuna, Tomato and Cashew Salad.
ABOVE: Crisp Garlic Sardines.

CHILLI AND CHUTNEY QUAIL WITH COUSCOUS SEASONING

12 quail
3/4 cup (180ml) mango chutney
2 tablespoons tomato paste
2 teaspoons sambal oelek
6 medium (1.2kg) tomatoes

COUSCOUS SEASONING
1/2 cup (100g) couscous
1/2 cup (125ml) boiling water
1 tablespoon olive oil
1 small (80g) onion, chopped
2 cloves garlic, crushed
2 teaspoons ground cumin
2 teaspoons ground coriander
1/2 teaspoon ground cinnamon
**1/3 cup (45g) slivered almonds,
    toasted**
**1 cup (230g) fresh dates, seeded,
    finely chopped**
**2 small (260g) tomatoes, seeded,
    finely chopped**

DRESSING
1 cup (250ml) plain yogurt
**1/3 cup chopped fresh
    coriander leaves**
1/3 cup chopped fresh mint
1 tablespoon seeded mustard
1 teaspoon sugar

Using scissors or sharp knife, cut along each side of quail backbone; remove and discard bone. Repeat process with remaining quail.

Place quail, skin side down, on board. Carefully cut through thigh joints and wing joints without cutting skin.

Scrape meat away from rib cage and breastbone; remove and discard bones. Fill quail with couscous seasoning, secure openings with toothpicks, tie legs together, tuck wings under.

Coat quail in combined chutney, paste and sambal oelek, place in large baking dish. Bake, uncovered, in moderately hot oven about 30 minutes or until tender. Quarter tomatoes, remove seeds; slice tomatoes. Serve quail on tomatoes; drizzle with dressing.

Couscous Seasoning: Combine couscous and water in medium bowl, stand 5 minutes or until water is absorbed. Heat oil in medium pan, add onion, garlic and spices, cook, stirring, until onion is soft. Remove from heat, add couscous and remaining ingredients; mix well.

Dressing: Blend or process all ingredients until smooth.

Serves 6.

- Couscous seasoning and dressing can be made a day ahead.
- Storage: Covered, separately, in refrigerator.
- Freeze: Not suitable.
- Microwave: Not suitable.

TAGINE OF BEEF WITH TOMATOES

1.5kg beef chuck steak
2 medium (600g) eggplants
coarse cooking salt
1/4 cup (60ml) olive oil
**2 medium (300g) onions,
    finely sliced**
3 cloves garlic, crushed
1 teaspoon ground turmeric
1 teaspoon ground coriander
1/2 teaspoon ground cinnamon
1/2 teaspoon ground ginger
2 teaspoons cumin seeds
2 1/2 cups (625ml) beef stock
**4 large (1kg) tomatoes,
    peeled, chopped**
1/2 cup (85g) seeded dates, halved
**2/3 cup (110g) blanched almonds,
    toasted**
2 tablespoons honey
**1/2 cup chopped fresh flat-leaf
    parsley**

Cut beef into 3cm pieces. Cut eggplants into 1cm slices, place in strainer, sprinkle with salt; stand 30 minutes. Rinse eggplant slices under cold water, drain, cut into quarters.

Heat half the oil in large pan, add beef in batches, cook until browned; drain on absorbent paper. Heat remaining oil in same pan, add onions, garlic and spices, cook, stirring, until onions are soft. Stir in stock, tomatoes and beef, simmer, covered, about 1 hour or until beef is just tender. Add eggplants, simmer, uncovered, about 30 minutes or until eggplants and beef are very tender. Stir in remaining ingredients.

Serves 6 to 8.

- Can be made a day ahead.
- Storage: Covered, in refrigerator.
- Freeze: Suitable.
- Microwave: Not suitable.

From back: Tagine of Beef with Tomatoes; Chilli and Chutney Quail with Couscous Seasoning.

Plates from The Bay Tree Kitchen Shop; tiles from Country Floors

LENTIL, TOMATO AND ROASTED VEGETABLE SALAD

3 large (1kg) red peppers
3 small (700g) eggplants
2 small (500g) kumara
coarse cooking salt
1/4 cup (60ml) light olive oil
1 bunch (500g) English spinach
250g cherry tomatoes, halved
330g yellow teardrop
   tomatoes, halved

LENTIL TOMATO TOPPING
1/2 cup (100g) red lentils
2 teaspoons light olive oil
1 medium (150g) onion,
   finely chopped
2 cloves garlic, crushed
1 1/2 teaspoons ground cumin
1/2 teaspoon ground allspice
2 tablespoons dried currants
6 medium (450g) egg
   tomatoes, chopped
1/4 cup chopped fresh mint
2 tablespoons chopped fresh
   coriander leaves

DRESSING
1/3 cup (80ml) lemon juice
1/2 cup (125ml) light olive oil
3 teaspoons sugar
2 teaspoons balsamic vinegar

Quarter peppers, remove seeds and membranes. Grill peppers, skin side up, until skin blisters and blackens. Peel away skin, slice peppers thickly. Cut eggplants and kumara into 1cm slices. Place eggplant slices in strainer, sprinkle with salt, stand 30 minutes.

Rinse eggplant slices under cold water, drain, pat dry with absorbent paper. Brush eggplant and kumara slices with oil, grill or barbecue until lightly browned and tender; cut slices in half. Discard stems from spinach.

Combine peppers, eggplants, kumara and tomatoes in large bowl; mix gently. Serve on spinach leaves with lentil tomato topping, drizzle with dressing.

Lentil Tomato Topping: Add lentils to medium pan of boiling water, simmer, uncovered, about 10 minutes or until just tender; drain. Heat oil in medium pan, add onion, garlic and spices, cook, stirring, until onion is soft. Add currants and lentils; cool 5 minutes. Combine lentil mixture with tomatoes and herbs; mix gently.

Dressing: Combine all ingredients in jar; shake well.

Serves 6.

■ Tomato and roasted vegetable salad best made just before serving. Dressing can be made a day ahead.
■ Storage: Covered, in refrigerator.
■ Freeze: Not suitable.
■ Microwave: Not suitable.

Tiles from Country Floors

BRAISED SPICED LAMB AND VEGETABLES

2 tablespoons olive oil
2kg leg of lamb
2 small (160g) onions, quartered
3 cloves garlic, crushed
2 large (700g) yellow peppers,
  roughly chopped
2 teaspoons ground cumin
2 teaspoons ground coriander
1/2 teaspoon ground sweet paprika
1/2 teaspoon ground turmeric
1/2 teaspoon ground cinnamon
6 medium (1.2kg) tomatoes,
  quartered
1kg baby new potatoes, halved
1 cup (250ml) dry red wine
1/2 cup (125ml) tomato paste
1/3 cup chopped fresh coriander
  leaves

Heat oil in large heavy-based pan, add lamb, cook until browned all over; drain on absorbent paper. Add onions, garlic, peppers and spices to pan, cook, stirring, until onions are soft. Return lamb to pan with remaining ingredients, simmer, covered, stirring occasionally, about 2 hours or until lamb is tender.

Remove lamb and vegetable mixture from pan, cover to keep warm. Simmer pan juices, uncovered, about 10 minutes or until reduced by half. Serve lamb and vegetable mixture drizzled with pan juices.

Serves 6 to 8.

■ Best made just before serving.
■ Freeze: Not suitable.
■ Microwave: Not suitable.

SUN-DRIED TOMATO AND SPINACH GNOCCHI

1 large (600g) bunch English
  spinach
1 tablespoon water
1 teaspoon olive oil
1 small (80g) onion, finely chopped
1/2 cup (75g) drained, finely chopped
  sun-dried tomatoes in oil
1 1/2 cups (300g) ricotta cheese
1 cup (80g) grated fresh
  parmesan cheese
2 egg yolks
3/4 teaspoon ground nutmeg
1 cup (150g) plain flour,
  approximately

CREAMY BACON SAUCE
1 small (80g) onion, finely chopped
2 bacon rashers, finely chopped
1 clove garlic, crushed
2 x 425g cans tomatoes
3/4 cup (180ml) cream
2 teaspoons sugar

Discard stems from spinach. Combine spinach and water in large pan, cook, covered, until just wilted; drain. Squeeze as much liquid as possible from spinach, finely chop spinach. Heat

China from Storehouse

oil in small pan, add onion, cook, stirring, until onion is soft; cool. Combine spinach, onion mixture, tomatoes, cheeses, egg yolks, nutmeg and enough sifted flour to mix to a soft dough.

Using floured hands, roll rounded teaspoons of mixture into ovals. Place an oval in palm of hand, press with floured fork to indent and flatten slightly. Repeat with remaining mixture. Place gnocchi on baking paper-covered trays as you make them. Add gnocchi to large pan of boiling water, boil, uncovered, about 2 minutes or until gnocchi float to the surface and are tender; drain. Serve gnocchi with creamy bacon sauce.

Creamy Bacon Sauce: Add onion, bacon and garlic to large pan, cook, stirring, until onion is soft and lightly browned. Press undrained tomatoes through fine sieve; discard pulp. Add tomato puree, cream and sugar to pan, simmer, uncovered, stirring occasionally, about 20 minutes or until thick.

Serves 4.

■ Gnocchi can be prepared 3 hours ahead. Sauce can be made a day ahead.
■ Storage: Gnocchi, in single layer on baking paper-covered oven trays, dusted with flour. Sauce, covered, in refrigerator.
■ Freeze: Not suitable.
■ Microwave: Gnocchi suitable.

LEFT: From back: Braised Spiced Lamb and Vegetables; Lentil, Tomato and Roasted Vegetable Salad.
ABOVE: Sun-Dried Tomato and Spinach Gnocchi.

From back: Seafood Paella; Baked Fish with Saute Vegetables.

BAKED FISH WITH SAUTE VEGETABLES

1 tablespoon olive oil
2 cloves garlic, crushed
2 tablespoons tomato paste
½ cup (125ml) dry white wine
2 tablespoons balsamic vinegar
1 cup (250ml) water
400g can tomatoes
2 tablespoons chopped fresh basil
2 teaspoons chopped fresh thyme
1kg snapper
4 sprigs fresh thyme
2 tablespoons lemon juice

SAUTE VEGETABLES
1 bunch (250g) asparagus
1 tablespoon olive oil
1 small (150g) red pepper, sliced
400g can artichoke hearts,
    drained, halved
2 large (180g) egg tomatoes, sliced

Heat oil in medium pan, add garlic, cook, stirring, until fragrant. Add paste, wine, vinegar, water and undrained crushed tomatoes, simmer, uncovered, about 5 minutes or until slightly thickened. Stir in chopped herbs.

Pour half the tomato mixture into shallow ovenproof dish (4 litre/16 cup) capacity. Cut 4 deep slits across each side of fish; place thyme sprigs in fish cavity. Place fish on tomato mixture in dish, pour over juice and remaining tomato mixture. Bake, uncovered, in moderate oven about 40 minutes or until fish is cooked. Remove from oven, cover with foil, stand 5 minutes. Serve fish and tomato mixture topped with saute vegetables.

Saute Vegetables: Snap off and discard tough ends of asparagus; chop asparagus. Heat oil in large pan, add asparagus and pepper, cook, stirring, until tender. Add artichokes and tomatoes, stir gently until hot.

Serves 2 to 4.

■ Best made just before serving.
■ Freeze: Not suitable.
■ Microwave: Suitable.

SEAFOOD PAELLA

 350g small mussels
12 (500g) uncooked medium prawns
¼ cup (60ml) olive oil
1 large (300g) red Spanish onion,
    thinly sliced
2 cloves garlic, crushed
1 medium (200g) yellow pepper,
    chopped
2 cups (400g) arborio rice
1 teaspoon ground sweet paprika
¼ teaspoon saffron powder
2¾ cups (680ml) fish stock
1 cup (250ml) dry white wine
2 tablespoons tomato paste
300g scallops
250g firm white fish fillets,
    thickly sliced
500g cherry tomatoes, halved

Scrub mussels, remove beards. Shell and devein prawns, leaving tails intact. Heat oil in large, wide pan, add onion and garlic, cook, stirring, until onion is soft. Add pepper, cook, stirring, 1 minute. Add rice and spices, cook, stirring, until fragrant.

Add 1 cup (250ml) of the combined stock and wine to rice mixture, cook, stirring, until liquid is absorbed. Add remaining stock mixture and paste, cook, stirring, until mixture boils. Place all seafood and tomatoes over rice mixture, simmer, covered, over low heat about 25 minutes or until liquid is absorbed. Remove from heat, stand, covered 5 minutes; stir gently with fork.

Serves 4 to 6.

■ Best made just before serving.
■ Freeze: Not suitable.
■ Microwave: Not suitable.

CHAR-GRILLED SALMON WITH CRISP FRIED CAPERS

11 medium (2kg) tomatoes, quartered
400g can artichoke hearts, drained, quartered
2½ cups (400g) seeded black olives
⅓ cup (80ml) olive oil
⅓ cup (55g) drained capers
8 x 150g salmon fillets
½ teaspoon cracked black peppercorns
½ teaspoon ground sweet paprika
½ teaspoon ground cumin

DRESSING
¼ cup (60ml) water
¼ cup firmly packed fresh basil leaves
2 tablespoons balsamic vinegar
2 teaspoons sugar
¾ cup (180ml) olive oil

Remove seeds from tomatoes, slice tomatoes thinly. Combine tomatoes, artichokes and olives with dressing in medium bowl; mix well. Heat oil in small pan, add capers, cook, stirring, until crisp and puffed; drain on absorbent paper. Sprinkle salmon with combined pepper and spices. Cook salmon in batches in heated greased griddle pan (or grill or barbecue) until browned and tender. Serve salmon with tomato salad; top with fried capers.

Dressing: Blend or process water, basil, vinegar and sugar until smooth. Add oil gradually in a thin stream while motor is operating.

Serves 8.

■ Best made close to serving.
■ Freeze: Not suitable.
■ Microwave: Not suitable.

CHAR-GRILLED CHICKEN WITH TOMATO MOLE

7 cloves garlic
2 teaspoons olive oil
1 small (80g) onion, finely chopped
3 fresh green poblano chillies, chopped
1 teaspoon ground coriander
½ teaspoon ground cinnamon
⅓ cup (25g) stale breadcrumbs, toasted
2 tablespoons blanched almonds, toasted, chopped
2 tablespoons unsalted roasted peanuts, chopped
¼ cup (40g) chopped raisins
3 medium (570g) tomatoes, peeled, seeded, chopped
1 tablespoon sesame seeds, toasted
2 cups (500ml) chicken stock
50g bittersweet chocolate, chopped
8 (1.4kg) chicken breast fillets

Wrap unpeeled garlic in foil, bake in hot oven about 20 minutes or until garlic is just soft. Peel garlic, chop roughly.

Heat oil in large pan, add onion, chillies and spices, cook, stirring, until onion is soft. Blend or process onion mixture, garlic, breadcrumbs, nuts, raisins, tomatoes, seeds and ⅓ cup (80ml) of the stock until almost smooth.

Return mixture to pan with remaining stock and chocolate, stir over low heat, without boiling, until chocolate is melted. Simmer, uncovered, about 10 minutes or until slightly thickened. Cook chicken in batches in heated greased griddle pan (or grill or barbecue) until browned and cooked through. Serve chicken with tomato mole.

Serves 8.

■ Tomato mole can be made a day ahead.
■ Storage: Covered, in refrigerator.
■ Freeze: Not suitable.
■ Microwave: Not suitable.

BEEF, BEAN AND CHORIZO SAUSAGE STEW

1.5kg beef chuck steak
¼ cup (60ml) olive oil
2 medium (300g) onions, sliced
4 cloves garlic, crushed
1 tablespoon ground hot paprika
2 (360g) chorizo sausages, sliced
¼ cup (60ml) tomato paste
2 x 400g cans tomatoes
2 tablespoons chopped fresh thyme
1 cup (250ml) dry red wine
**2 x 300g cans butter beans,
  rinsed, drained**

Cut beef into 3cm pieces. Heat 2 tablespoons of the oil in large pan, add beef in batches, cook, stirring, until browned; remove from pan. Heat remaining oil in same pan, add onions, garlic, paprika and sausages, cook, stirring, until onions are soft. Return beef to pan, stir in paste, undrained crushed tomatoes, thyme and wine, simmer, covered, about 1½ hours or until beef is tender, stirring occasionally. Remove lid, simmer about 30 minutes or until thickened slightly; stir occasionally. Add beans, stir until hot.

Serves 6.

■ Can be made a day ahead.
■ Storage: Covered, in refrigerator.
■ Freeze: Suitable.
■ Microwave: Not suitable.

LEFT: Char-Grilled Salmon with Crisp Fried Capers.
ABOVE: From back: Beef, Bean and Chorizo Sausage Stew; Char-Grilled Chicken with Tomato Mole.

MARINATED BEEF AND NOODLE SALAD

750g beef eye-fillet steaks
2 tablespoons fish sauce
1 tablespoon mild curry powder
1/4 cup chopped fresh coriander
   leaves
1/4 cup chopped fresh mint
2 small fresh red chillies, chopped
2 cloves garlic, crushed
2 tablespoons peanut oil
2 tablespoons chopped fresh
   lemon grass
375g packet thick rice stick noodles
3 medium (360g) carrots
3 small (400g) Lebanese cucumbers
250g sugar snap peas
6 medium (1.2kg) tomatoes,
   quartered, seeded

DRESSING
2 medium (380g) tomatoes,
   chopped
1/3 cup (80ml) lime juice
2 cloves garlic, chopped
2 tablespoons chopped fresh mint
1/3 cup (80ml) peanut oil

Combine beef, sauce, curry powder, herbs, chillies, garlic, oil and lemon grass in large bowl, cover, refrigerate 3 hours or overnight.

Place noodles in large bowl, cover with boiling water, stand 20 minutes, drain; rinse under cold water, drain well. Drain beef from marinade. Cook beef in batches in heated greased griddle pan (or grill or barbecue) until browned and tender, stand 10 minutes before slicing thinly.

Using a vegetable peeler, cut carrots into very thin strips. Halve cucumbers lengthways, remove seeds, slice cucumbers. Add peas to medium pan of boiling water, drain immediately, rinse under cold water; drain well. Combine noodles, beef, tomatoes, carrots, cucumbers and peas in large bowl, add dressing, stir gently until combined.

Dressing: Blend or process all ingredients until smooth.

Serves 6.

■ Best made just before serving.
■ Freeze: Not suitable.
■ Microwave: Not suitable.

TOMATO GINGER-GLAZED FISH CUTLETS

We used blue-eyed cod for this recipe.

2 teaspoons peanut oil
2 tablespoons grated fresh ginger
2 cloves garlic, crushed
1 small fresh red chilli, sliced
2 tablespoons lime juice
1 tablespoon green ginger wine
1/4 cup (55g) sugar
1 tablespoon tomato paste
1/2 cup (125ml) orange juice
3/4 cup (180ml) tomato juice
4 (1kg) white fish cutlets

Heat oil in small pan, add ginger, garlic and chilli, cook, stirring, until fragrant. Add juice and wine, simmer, uncovered, until almost all liquid has evaporated. Add sugar, cook, stirring, without boiling, until sugar is dissolved. Stir in paste and juices, simmer, uncovered, without stirring, about 7 minutes or until thickened slightly; cool.

Combine fish with half the sauce mixture in medium bowl, cover, refrigerate 3 hours or overnight.

Drain fish; discard marinade. Cook fish in batches in heated greased griddle pan (or grill or barbecue) until browned on both sides and cooked through. Heat remaining sauce mixture in small pan, serve with fish cutlets.

Serves 4.

■ Sauce mixture can be made
   a day ahead. Fish can be
   prepared a day ahead.
■ Storage: Covered, separately,
   in refrigerator.
■ Freeze: Not suitable.
■ Microwave: Not suitable.

Fabric from Orson & Blake Collectables; small box from Corso de' Fiori

LAMB FILLETS WITH ROASTED VEGETABLES

6 medium (450g) egg tomatoes
2 small (120g) finger eggplants
2 small (180g) zucchini
1 small (150g) red pepper, quartered
8 small (100g) yellow squash, halved
4 baby (100g) onions, halved
2 cloves garlic, unpeeled
1/4 cup (60ml) olive oil
1/2 teaspoon cracked black peppercorns
1/4 teaspoon fennel seeds
1/2 teaspoon sugar
8 (640g) lamb fillets

PESTO
2 cups firmly packed fresh basil leaves
1/4 cup (40g) pine nuts, toasted
1/4 cup (20g) grated fresh parmesan cheese
1/4 cup (60ml) olive oil

Cut tomatoes, eggplants and zucchini in half lengthways. Place tomatoes, eggplants, zucchini, red pepper, squash, onions and garlic in large baking dish, drizzle with oil, sprinkle with black pepper, seeds and sugar. Bake, uncovered, in hot oven about 1 1/4 hours or until vegetables are very soft.

Cook lamb in batches in heated greased griddle pan (or grill or barbecue) until browned and cooked as desired. Serve sliced lamb with roasted vegetables and pesto.

Pesto: Blend or process basil, nuts and cheese until chopped. Add oil gradually in a thin stream while motor is operating, blend until thick and smooth.

Serves 4 to 6.

■ Pesto can be made a day ahead.
■ Storage: Covered, in refrigerator.
■ Freeze: Not suitable.
■ Microwave: Not suitable.

SPICY SAUSAGE AND BEAN BAKE

We used French tomato sausages but any fresh, spicy sausages are suitable.

2 medium (400g) red peppers
1 tablespoon olive oil
800g fresh spicy sausages
2 medium (300g) onions, sliced
3 cloves garlic, crushed
1 bacon rasher, chopped
310g can butter beans, rinsed, drained
400g can tomatoes
1 tablespoon tomato paste
1/4 cup (60ml) Worcestershire sauce

CRUMB TOPPING
2 cups (140g) stale breadcrumbs
1 cup (80g) coarsely grated fresh parmesan cheese
60g butter, melted
1/3 cup chopped fresh parsley

Plates from The Bay Tree Kitchen Shop

Quarter peppers, remove seeds and membranes. Grill peppers, skin side up, until skin blisters and blackens. Peel away skin, chop peppers. Heat oil in large pan, add sausages, cook until browned and cooked through. Remove from pan, cool 5 minutes; roughly chop sausages.

Drain all but 1 tablespoon of the oil from pan. Add onions, garlic and bacon to pan, cook, stirring, until onions are soft. Add peppers, sausages, beans, undrained crushed tomatoes, paste and sauce. Spoon sausage mixture into shallow ovenproof dish (2 litre/8 cup capacity); sprinkle with crumb topping. Bake in moderately hot oven about

30 minutes or until crumb topping is lightly browned.

Crumb Topping: Combine all ingredients in small bowl; mix well.

Serves 4.

■ Recipe can be made a day ahead.
■ Storage: Covered, in refrigerator.
■ Freeze: Not suitable.
■ Microwave: Not suitable.

LEFT: From left: Marinated Beef and Noodle Salad; Tomato Ginger-Glazed Fish Cutlets.
ABOVE: From back: Spicy Sausage and Bean Bake; Lamb Fillets with Roasted Vegetables.

SPAGHETTI BOLOGNESE

1 tablespoon olive oil
1 large (200g) onion, chopped
2 cloves garlic, crushed
1kg minced beef
6 medium (1.2kg) tomatoes,
  peeled, chopped
425g can tomato puree
1/3 cup (80ml) tomato paste
1 cup (250ml) beef stock
1/2 cup (125ml) dry red wine
1 teaspoon sugar
2 tablespoons chopped fresh basil
2 tablespoons chopped fresh
  parsley
500g spaghetti

Heat oil in medium pan, add onion and
garlic, cook, stirring, until onion is soft.
Add beef, cook, stirring, until beef is
well browned. Stir in tomatoes, puree,
paste, stock, wine and sugar, simmer,
uncovered, about 1 hour or until thick.
Stir in herbs.

Meanwhile, add pasta to large pan of
boiling water, boil, uncovered, until just
tender; drain. Serve bolognese sauce
over pasta.

Serves 4 to 6.

■ Bolognese sauce can be made
  a day ahead.
■ Storage: Covered, in refrigerator.
■ Freeze: Suitable.
■ Microwave: Pasta suitable.

VEAL PARMIGIANA

6 (860g) veal leg steaks
plain flour
1 egg, lightly beaten
1/2 cup (125ml) milk
1 1/2 cups (150g) packaged
  breadcrumbs
vegetable oil for frying
6 slices (90g) prosciutto
12 large fresh basil leaves
100g mozzarella cheese,
  thinly sliced

TOMATO SAUCE
1 tablespoon olive oil
1 medium (150g) onion, chopped
2 cloves garlic, crushed
4 medium (760g) tomatoes,
  peeled, chopped
2 tablespoons tomato paste
1 tablespoon chopped fresh
  oregano leaves
2 tablespoons balsamic vinegar

Coat veal in flour, shake away excess
flour, dip into combined egg and milk,
then into breadcrumbs. Place on tray,
cover, refrigerate 00 minutes.

Fry veal in batches in a little hot oil
until browned and just cooked through;
drain on absorbent paper. Place veal in
single layer on oven tray, spoon over
tomato sauce, top with prosciutto
slices, basil leaves and cheese. Grill
until cheese is melted.

Tomato Sauce: Heat oil in pan, add
onion and garlic, cook, stirring, until
onion is soft. Add tomatoes, paste,
oregano and vinegar, simmer, uncovered, about 5 minutes or until thick.

Serves 6.
■ Veal can be prepared a day ahead.
  Sauce can be made a day ahead.
■ Storage: Covered, separately,
  in refrigerator.
■ Freeze: Sauce suitable.
■ Microwave: Not suitable.

*ABOVE: From left: Spaghetti Bolognese;
Veal Parmigiana.*
RIGHT: Tomato Prawn Curry.

TOMATO PRAWN CURRY

1kg uncooked medium prawns
400ml can coconut milk
½ cup (125ml) water
¼ cup (60ml) fish sauce
2 fresh kaffir lime leaves, halved
2 teaspoons sugar
½ bunch (250g) English spinach, roughly chopped
¼ cup loosely packed fresh coriander leaves
1kg packet thick fresh rice noodles

SPICY TOMATO SAUCE
4 medium (800g) tomatoes, halved
3 cloves garlic, crushed
1 large (200g) onion, finely chopped
1 stem lemon grass, finely chopped
¼ cup (60ml) lime juice
2 tablespoons peanut oil

1 tablespoon finely chopped fresh coriander root
2 teaspoons grated fresh ginger
2 teaspoons dried crushed chillies
2 teaspoons ground turmeric
1 teaspoon belacan
1 teaspoon ground cumin

Shell and devein prawns, leaving tails intact; flatten prawns slightly. Combine spicy tomato sauce, coconut milk, water, fish sauce, lime leaves and sugar in large pan, stir over low heat, without boiling, about 10 minutes. Stir in prawns and spinach, simmer, uncovered, about 5 minutes or until prawns are tender; stir in coriander. Place noodles in large bowl, cover with boiling water, stand 5 minutes; drain. Serve tomato prawn curry with noodles.

Spicy Tomato Sauce: Combine all ingredients in large baking dish, bake, uncovered, in very hot oven about 30 minutes or until tomatoes are pulpy. Blend or process tomato mixture until smooth.

Serves 4 to 6.

- Best made just before serving. Spicy tomato sauce can be made a day ahead.
- Storage: Covered, in refrigerator.
- Freeze: Not suitable.
- Microwave: Not suitable.

Plates from Orson & Blake Collectables

91

Side Dishes

The natural sweetness and freshness of tomatoes perfectly complement salads, tarts, polenta and all manner of vegetables. Here, you'll find the best ever green tomato fritters, a hearty gratin of tomato and potato and flavourful salads. Many recipes could double as light main meals.

GRILLED EGGPLANT AND TOMATO STACKS

2 large (1kg) eggplants
coarse cooking salt
¼ cup (60ml) olive oil
6 medium (450g) egg tomatoes
60g butter
2 cups (140g) stale breadcrumbs
2 teaspoons chopped fresh thyme
1 tablespoon chopped fresh oregano leaves
2 tablespoons balsamic vinegar

Cut eggplants into 1cm slices, place on wire racks, sprinkle with salt, stand 30 minutes. Rinse slices under cold water; drain on absorbent paper. Brush slices on both sides with some of the oil, cook in batches in heated griddle pan until browned on both sides and tender; drain on absorbent paper. Cover slices to keep warm.

Cut tomatoes into 1cm slices lengthways, brush both sides with more of the oil. Cook tomatoes in batches in same pan until slightly softened. Cover to keep warm.

Melt butter in medium pan, add breadcrumbs and herbs, cook, stirring, until lightly browned and crisp. Place a slice of eggplant on each plate, top with 3 slices of tomato. Repeat layers, finishing with eggplant. Drizzle stacks with vinegar, sprinkle with crispy breadcrumb mixture.

Serves 6.
- Best made just before serving.
- Freeze: Not suitable.
- Microwave: Not suitable.

PEPPER, TOMATO AND CRUNCHY BREAD SALAD

We used about a quarter of the pagnotta in this recipe. Any type of dry Italian-style bread could be used.

1 medium (70g) bulb garlic
9 medium (675g) egg tomatoes, peeled
¼ cup (60ml) olive oil
1 pagnotta
2 tablespoons olive oil, extra
2 large (700g) red peppers
1 large (350g) yellow pepper
1 cup lightly packed large fresh basil leaves, torn

DRESSING
2 tablespoons red wine vinegar
2 teaspoons brown sugar
⅓ cup (80ml) olive oil

Separate garlic bulb into cloves. Combine garlic, tomatoes and oil in baking dish. Bake, uncovered, in moderately hot oven about 30 minutes, or until tomatoes are soft, gently turning tomatoes occasionally; cool. Reserve garlic for dressing.

Cut bread into 2cm squares, combine in bowl with extra oil; mix well. Place bread in single layer on oven tray, toast in moderate oven about 10 minutes.

Quarter peppers, remove seeds and membranes. Grill peppers, skin side up, until skin blisters and blackens. Peel away skin, slice peppers into thick strips. Combine tomatoes, peppers, basil and dressing in large bowl; toss gently. Add crunchy bread to salad just before serving.

Dressing: Squeeze pulp from reserved garlic. Blend or process pulp with vinegar and sugar until smooth. Add oil gradually in a thin stream while motor is operating, blend until thick.

Serves 4 to 6.
- Crunchy bread and dressing can be made a day ahead.
- Storage: Dressing, covered, in refrigerator. Crunchy bread, in airtight container.
- Freeze: Not suitable.
- Microwave: Not suitable.

From back: Pepper, Tomato and Crunchy Bread Salad; Grilled Eggplant and Tomato Stacks.

TOMATO AND BLACK-EYED BEAN SALAD

1¼ cups (250g) dried
  black-eyed beans
2 green shallots, chopped
2 medium (380g) tomatoes,
  chopped
330g yellow teardrop tomatoes,
  halved
1 stick celery, sliced
2 tablespoons chopped fresh basil
2 tablespoons chopped fresh mint
1 bunch (120g) rocket

DRESSING
⅓ cup (80ml) olive oil
1 tablespoon white wine vinegar
1 teaspoon mild English mustard
½ teaspoon cracked black
  peppercorns
2 tablespoons lemon juice

Place beans in large bowl, cover with cold water, cover, stand overnight.

Drain beans, add to pan of boiling water, simmer, uncovered, about 30 minutes or until beans are tender; drain. Combine beans, shallots, tomatoes, celery, herbs and torn rocket leaves in large bowl, drizzle with dressing; mix gently.
Dressing: Combine all ingredients in jar; shake well.

Serves 4 to 6.

■ Best made just before serving.
■ Freeze: Not suitable.
■ Microwave: Not suitable.

SILVERBEET WITH TOMATOES AND SLICED GARLIC

2 tablespoons olive oil
10 medium (750g) egg tomatoes,
  halved lengthways
2 medium (300g) onions, sliced
4 cloves garlic, sliced
1 bunch (1kg) silverbeet, shredded
½ cup (125ml) vegetable stock
1 tablespoon tomato paste
2 tablespoons lemon juice
½ cup (125ml) cream
1 teaspoon sambal oelek

Heat half the oil in large pan, add tomatoes in batches, cook until slightly softened; remove from pan. Heat remaining oil in same pan, add onions and garlic, cook, stirring, until onions are soft. Add silverbeet and stock, cook, stirring, until silverbeet is wilted. Stir in combined paste, juice, cream and sambal oelek, stir over heat until mixture boils and thickens slightly. Add tomatoes, mix gently.

Serves 4 to 6.

■ Best made just before serving.
■ Freeze: Not suitable.
■ Microwave: Not suitable.

FRUIT AND NUT COUSCOUS WITH ROASTED TOMATOES

8 medium (600g) egg tomatoes,
  halved lengthways
1 teaspoon salt
2 cups (400g) couscous
2 cups (500ml) boiling water
30g butter, chopped
1 tablespoon olive oil
5 medium (750g) onions, sliced
1 clove garlic, crushed
2 teaspoons ground cumin
2 teaspoons ground coriander
½ teaspoon ground sweet paprika
½ teaspoon ground cinnamon
⅓ cup (75g) sugar
1 tablespoon white vinegar
⅓ cup (45g) slivered almonds,
  toasted
½ cup (75g) dried apricots, halved
1 cup (230g) fresh dates,
  seeded, halved
¼ cup chopped fresh coriander
  leaves

Place tomatoes, cut side up, on wire rack over baking dish, sprinkle with salt. Bake, uncovered, in hot oven about 50 minutes or until soft; cover to keep warm. Combine couscous, water and butter in bowl, stand 5 minutes or until water is absorbed. Fluff couscous with a fork.

Heat oil in large heavy-based pan, add onions, garlic and spices, cook, stirring, 5 minutes. Add sugar and vinegar, cook, stirring, about 15 minutes or until onions are caramelised. Add couscous, nuts, fruit and coriander, stir gently until hot. Serve fruit and nut couscous with roasted tomatoes.

Serves 6.

■ Best made just before serving.
■ Freeze: Not suitable.
■ Microwave: Not suitable.

LEFT: From left: Silverbeet with Tomatoes and Sliced Garlic; Tomato and Black-Eyed Bean Salad.
BELOW: Fruit and Nut Couscous with Roasted Tomatoes.

Placemat from Home & Garden on the Mall

TOMATO BOCCONCINI SALAD

350g bocconcini cheese, sliced
3 medium (570g) tomatoes, sliced
½ small (50g) red Spanish onion, thinly sliced
¾ cup loosely packed fresh basil leaves

DRESSING
¼ cup (60ml) balsamic vinegar
¼ cup (60ml) olive oil
½ teaspoon cracked black peppercorns
1 tablespoon chopped fresh oregano leaves

Layer cheese, tomatoes, onion and basil on platter; drizzle with dressing.
Dressing: Combine all ingredients in jar; shake well.

Serves 6.
■ Can be made 3 hours ahead.
■ Storage: Covered, separately, in refrigerator.
■ Freeze: Not suitable.

WARM CARAMELISED TOMATO AND ONION SALAD

4 medium (800g) yellow peppers
1 tablespoon olive oil
4 medium (600g) onions, sliced
¼ cup chopped fresh basil
2 tablespoons balsamic vinegar
4 medium (300g) egg tomatoes, chopped
2 tablespoons brown sugar
⅓ cup (25g) flaked fresh parmesan cheese

Quarter peppers, remove seeds and membranes. Grill peppers, skin side up, until skin blisters and blackens. Peel away skin.

Heat oil in pan, add onions, cook, stirring, until onions are soft. Add basil, vinegar and tomatoes, cook, stirring, until tomatoes are soft. Add sugar, stir until sugar is dissolved. Place quarter of the peppers on plate, top with quarter of the onion mixture and a little cheese. Continue layering with remaining ingredients.

Serves 4.
■ Best made just before serving.
■ Freeze: Not suitable.
■ Microwave: Not suitable.

SPICED POTATOES WITH ROASTED TOMATO RELISH

6 medium (1.2kg) potatoes
1 teaspoon cumin seeds
1 teaspoon ground hot paprika
1 teaspoon dried oregano leaves
2 tablespoons olive oil

ROASTED TOMATO RELISH
1 large (350g) red pepper
2 tablespoons olive oil
10 medium (750g) egg tomatoes,
   halved lengthways
1 medium (150g) onion, chopped
2 cloves garlic, crushed
½ teaspoon yellow mustard seeds
½ teaspoon black mustard seeds
1 tablespoon balsamic vinegar
2 tablespoons sugar
1 teaspoon salt

Cut potatoes in half, cut each half into 4 wedges. Combine wedges with remaining ingredients in large baking dish; mix well. Bake, uncovered, in moderately hot oven about 1 hour or until potatoes are browned and crisp. Serve with roasted tomato relish.

Roasted Tomato Relish: Quarter pepper, remove seeds and membranes. Grill pepper, skin side up, until skin blisters and blackens. Peel away skin, chop pepper finely.

Pour half the oil into large baking dish, add tomatoes in single layer. Bake, uncovered, in slow oven about 1½ hours or until tomatoes are soft. Heat remaining oil in medium pan, add onion, garlic and seeds, cook, stirring, until onion is soft. Stir in pepper, tomatoes, vinegar, sugar and salt, simmer, covered, about 15 minutes or until relish is thick.

Serves 4 to 6.

■ Relish can be made 2 days ahead.
■ Storage: Covered, in refrigerator.
■ Freeze: Not suitable.
■ Microwave: Not suitable.

Plate, platter and salt and pepper containers from Bayteak; corkscrew from Home & Garden on the Mall; tiles from Country Floors

Pewterware from Home & Garden on the Mall; glass stand from Made on Earth

LEFT: From back: Tomato Bocconcini Salad; Warm Caramelised Tomato and Onion Salad.
RIGHT: Spiced Potatoes with Roasted Tomato Relish.

TOMATO AND PEACH SALAD

2 large pita pocket breads
1 tablespoon olive oil
2 small (260g) Lebanese cucumbers
1 medium (170g) red Spanish onion
4 medium (800g) slipstone peaches
6 medium (450g) egg tomatoes
2 tablespoons chopped fresh mint
2 tablespoons chopped fresh
   coriander leaves

DRESSING
1/4 cup (60ml) lemon juice
1/3 cup (80ml) olive oil
3 teaspoons white wine vinegar
1 teaspoon ground cumin
1 clove garlic, crushed
3 teaspoons sugar

Brush bread on both sides with oil, place on oven trays. Toast in moderately hot oven about 15 minutes or until crisp, cool. Break bread into pieces. Cut cucumbers in half lengthways, scoop out seeds, slice cucumbers thinly. Cut onion in half, cut each half into 6 wedges.

Cut a shallow cross in base of each peach, drop peaches into large pan of boiling water, drain, rinse under cold water; drain. Cut peaches in half, twist peaches to remove stones; peel. Cut peaches and tomatoes into wedges. Combine cucumbers, onion, peaches, tomatoes and herbs in large bowl. Just before serving, add crispy bread; drizzle with dressing.

Dressing: Combine all ingredients in jar; shake well.

Serves 6.

▨ Bread and dressing can be made a day ahead.
▨ Storage: Bread, in airtight container. Dressing, covered, in refrigerator.
▨ Freeze: Not suitable.
▨ Microwave: Not suitable.

CARAMELISED ONION AND TOMATO TART

1 sheet ready-rolled puff pastry
1 egg, lightly beaten
125g cherry tomatoes, halved
165g yellow teardrop tomatoes,
halved
1/3 cup (25g) flaked fresh
parmesan cheese
1 tablespoon shredded fresh basil

CARAMELISED ONIONS
30g butter
1 tablespoon olive oil
3 medium (450g) onions,
thinly sliced
2 tablespoons brown vinegar
1 tablespoon sugar

Cut 24cm round from pastry sheet, place on greased oven tray, pinch pastry edge to make a 1cm rim. Cover pastry with baking paper, fill with dried beans or rice. Bake in very hot oven 15 minutes, remove paper and beans. Brush pastry with egg, bake in very hot oven about 5 minutes or until crisp.

Spoon hot caramelised onions onto pastry, top with combined tomatoes; sprinkle with cheese. Bake in very hot oven about 5 minutes or until tomatoes are just soft. Sprinkle with basil.

Caramelised Onions: Heat butter and oil in medium pan, add onions, cook, stirring, over low heat about 15 minutes or until onions are very soft. Add vinegar and sugar, cook, stirring, until onions are caramelised.

Serves 4 to 6.
■ Best made just before serving.
■ Freeze: Not suitable.
■ Microwave: Not suitable.

OLIVE AND SUN-DRIED TOMATO POLENTA

1 litre (4 cups) chicken stock
1 cup (170g) polenta
1 cup (200g) coarsely crumbled
feta cheese
2/3 cup (50g) coarsely grated fresh
parmesan cheese
1/2 cup firmly packed fresh basil
leaves, roughly chopped
1/3 cup (40g) seeded black
olives, halved
2/3 cup (100g) drained sun-dried
tomatoes in oil, chopped
plain flour
vegetable oil for frying

Lightly grease 20cm round sandwich cake pan. Bring stock to boil in large pan, add polenta, simmer, stirring, about 15 minutes or until polenta is very thick. Remove polenta from heat, stir in cheeses, basil, olives and tomatoes. Press polenta mixture firmly into prepared pan, cool to room temperature; refrigerate 3 hours or until firm.

Cut polenta into 16 wedges. Toss polenta in flour, shake away excess flour. Fry polenta in a large pan in a little hot oil until lightly browned and crisp; drain on absorbent paper.

Makes 16.
■ Polenta can be prepared a day ahead.
■ Storage: Covered, in refrigerator.
■ Freeze: Not suitable.
■ Microwave: Not suitable.

LEFT: Tomato and Peach Salad.
BELOW: From left: Caramelised Onion and Tomato Tart; Olive and Sun-Dried Tomato Polenta.

TOMATO AND POTATO AU GRATIN

3 medium (600g) potatoes, peeled
5 small (650g) tomatoes
40g butter
¼ cup (35g) plain flour
1 cup (250ml) milk
½ cup (125ml) chicken stock
1 teaspoon chopped fresh thyme
½ cup (60g) grated gruyere cheese

Grease shallow ovenproof dish (1.5 litre/ 6 cup capacity). Cut potatoes and tomatoes into 5mm slices. Boil or steam potatoes until tender. Melt butter in medium pan, stir in flour, stir over heat until bubbling. Remove from heat, gradually stir in milk and stock, stir over heat until sauce boils and thickens. Remove from heat, stir in thyme and half the cheese.

Overlap half the potatoes and tomatoes in prepared dish; spread with two-thirds of the sauce. Overlap remaining potatoes and tomatoes in dish, top with remaining sauce, sprinkle with remaining cheese. Bake in moderate oven about 20 minutes or until lightly browned and heated through.

Serves 4.
■ Can be prepared 3 hours ahead.
■ Storage: Covered, in refrigerator.
■ Freeze: Not suitable.
■ Microwave: Sauce suitable.

PARSLEY AND CORIANDER TOMATO SALAD

½ cup (80g) burghul
250g cherry tomatoes, halved
330g yellow teardrop tomatoes, halved
1 cup loosely packed fresh coriander leaves, finely chopped
2 cups loosely packed flat-leaf parsley, finely chopped
5 green shallots, finely chopped
1 medium (150g) red Spanish onion, finely chopped

DRESSING
2 small fresh red chillies, finely chopped
1 teaspoon ground cumin
⅓ cup (80ml) lemon juice
½ cup (125ml) olive oil

Place burghul in medium bowl, cover with cold water, stand 30 minutes. Drain burghul, rinse under cold water, drain; blot dry with absorbent paper. Combine burghul with remaining ingredients in bowl, add dressing; mix gently.
Dressing: Combine all ingredients in jar; shake well.

Serves 4 to 6.
■ Best made on day of serving.
■ Storage: Covered, in refrigerator.
■ Freeze: Not suitable.

OLIVE, ONION AND TOMATO SALAD

8 medium (1.5kg) tomatoes
1 large (300g) red Spanish onion, sliced
2 cups (320g) seeded black olives
1 cup firmly packed fresh basil leaves, shredded

DRESSING
¼ cup (60ml) olive oil
1 tablespoon balsamic vinegar
½ teaspoon sugar
1 tablespoon seeded mustard

Quarter tomatoes lengthways, remove seeds; slice each quarter in half lengthways. Combine tomatoes with remaining ingredients in bowl, add dressing; mix gently.
Dressing: Combine all ingredients in jar; shake well.

Serves 6.
■ Best made just before serving.
■ Freeze: Not suitable.

LEFT: From left: Parsley and Coriander Tomato Salad; Tomato and Potato au Gratin.
BELOW: Olive, Onion and Tomato Salad.

TOMATO CUPS WITH RICE AND BACON FILLING

8 medium (1.5kg) tomatoes
¼ cup (45g) wild rice
¼ cup (50g) basmati rice
2 bacon rashers, finely chopped
1 medium (170g) red Spanish onion, chopped
⅓ cup (25g) coarsely grated fresh parmesan cheese

PESTO
1½ cups firmly packed fresh basil
2 cloves garlic, chopped
2 tablespoons pine nuts, toasted
2 tablespoons olive oil

Cut tops from tomatoes; discard tops. Slightly trim bases to sit flat. Scoop out seeds and pulp from tomatoes; reserve for another use. Add wild rice to medium pan of boiling water, boil, uncovered, 10 minutes. Add basmati rice to same pan, boil, uncovered, further 12 minutes or until rice is tender; drain.

Add bacon and onion to medium pan, cook, stirring, until bacon is crisp. Combine rice mixture, bacon mixture, pesto and half the cheese in bowl. Spoon rice mixture into tomato shells, place in shallow ovenproof dish; sprinkle with remaining cheese. Bake, uncovered, in moderate oven about 20 minutes or until hot.

Pesto: Process basil, garlic and nuts until ingredients are finely chopped. Add oil in a thin stream while motor is operating, process until smooth.

Makes 8.

■ Can be prepared 3 hours ahead.
■ Storage: Covered, in refrigerator.
■ Freeze: Not suitable.
■ Microwave: Rice and tomatoes suitable.

MIXED LEAF AND TOMATO SALAD WITH TOASTED NUTS

150g mixed baby salad leaves
⅓ cup firmly packed fresh coriander leaves, chopped
250g cherry tomatoes
330g yellow teardrop tomatoes
1 large (300g) red Spanish onion, thinly sliced
1 cup (100g) walnuts, toasted

DRESSING
2 tablespoons balsamic vinegar
2 tablespoons lemon juice
1 tablespoon tomato paste
¼ cup (60ml) olive oil
1 teaspoon ground cumin
2 teaspoons sambal oelek

Combine all ingredients in large bowl, add dressing; mix gently.
Dressing: Combine all ingredients in jar; shake well.

Serves 6.

■ Best made just before serving. Dressing can be made a day ahead.
■ Storage: Covered, in refrigerator.
■ Freeze: Not suitable.

Plate and bowl from Storehouse

LEFT: From back: Tomato Cups with Rice and Bacon Filling; Mixed Leaf and Tomato Salad with Toasted Nuts.
RIGHT: Clockwise from back: Green Tomato Fritters; Soft Polenta with Herbs; Saute Mushrooms with Mint Butter.

Plates, bowl, trivet and cutlery from Ventura Design

SAUTE MUSHROOMS WITH MINT BUTTER

20g butter
1 tablespoon olive oil
1 clove garlic, crushed
200g oyster mushrooms
100g shiitake mushrooms, halved
200g button mushrooms, halved
250g cherry tomatoes, halved

MINT BUTTER
60g butter
1 tablespoon chopped fresh mint
1 tablespoon lemon juice
½ teaspoon cracked black peppercorns

Heat butter and oil in medium pan, add garlic, cook until fragrant. Add mushrooms and tomatoes, cook, stirring gently, about 4 minutes or until mushrooms have softened slightly; drizzle with mint butter.
Mint Butter: Melt butter in small pan, stir in remaining ingredients.

Serves 4.

▧ Best made just before serving.
▧ Freeze: Not suitable.
▧ Microwave: Mint butter suitable.

SOFT POLENTA WITH HERBS

1 litre (4 cups) chicken stock
¾ cup (125g) polenta
½ cup (125ml) cream
½ cup (40g) coarsely grated fresh parmesan cheese
3 medium (550g) tomatoes, peeled, seeded, finely chopped
1 tablespoon chopped fresh parsley
2 teaspoons finely chopped fresh sage

Bring stock to boil in large pan, add polenta, simmer, stirring, about 30 minutes or until mixture is soft and thick. Add remaining ingredients, stir until mixture is hot. Serve with meat or vegetables, or as a dip.

Makes about 1 litre (4 cups).

▧ Best made just before serving.
▧ Freeze: Not suitable.
▧ Microwave: Not suitable.

GREEN TOMATO FRITTERS

4 medium (760g) green tomatoes
plain flour
1 egg, lightly beaten
¼ cup (60ml) milk
1½ cups (255g) cornmeal
vegetable oil for shallow-frying
6 slices (90g) pancetta

GARLIC MAYONNAISE
2 cloves garlic, roughly chopped
2 egg yolks
1 cup (250ml) light olive oil
½ teaspoon dried crushed chillies
2 tablespoons water
1 tablespoon lemon juice

Cut tomatoes into 5mm slices. Toss slices in flour, shake away excess flour, dip in combined egg and milk, then cornmeal. Shallow-fry tomato slices in batches in hot oil until browned on both sides; drain on absorbent paper. Grill pancetta until crisp. Serve fritters with pancetta and garlic mayonnaise.
Garlic Mayonnaise: Blend or process garlic and egg yolks until smooth. Add oil gradually in a thin stream while motor is operating; stir in remaining ingredients.

Serves 6 to 8.

▧ Fritters best made just before serving. Garlic mayonnaise can be made a day ahead.
▧ Storage: Covered, in refrigerator.
▧ Freeze: Not suitable.
▧ Microwave: Not suitable.

Baking

Golden breads and rolls fresh from the oven are even more delicious with the taste of tomatoes. Many of these treats are substantial, others are light – all make perfect portable food and are great for picnics, lunch-boxes and snacks.

SUN-DRIED CAPSICUM AND TOMATO FOCACCIAS

2 tablespoons olive oil
1 large (200g) onion, sliced
1/4 cup shredded fresh basil
2 tablespoons drained, chopped
    sun-dried capsicums in oil
1/4 cup (35g) drained, chopped
    sun-dried tomatoes in oil
2 teaspoons (7g) dry yeast
2 teaspoons sugar
1/2 cup (125ml) warm water
3 1/2 cups (525g) plain flour
1 teaspoon table salt
1/2 cup (125ml) warm water,
    approximately, extra
1 clove garlic, crushed
1 teaspoon fine sea salt
1/2 teaspoon poppy seeds

Heat half the oil in pan, add onion, cook, stirring, until onion is soft. Remove from heat, stir in basil, capsicums and tomatoes; cool.

Combine yeast, sugar, water and 1 tablespoon of the flour in small bowl, whisk until yeast is dissolved. Cover, stand in warm place about 15 minutes or until mixture is frothy.

Sift remaining flour and table salt into large bowl, stir in onion mixture, yeast mixture and enough extra water to mix to a soft dough. Turn dough onto floured surface, knead about 10 minutes or until smooth and elastic. Place

dough in greased bowl, cover, stand in warm place about 40 minutes or until dough has doubled in size.

Knead dough on floured surface until smooth. Divide dough into 4 pieces, roll each piece to a 15cm round. Place rounds on greased oven trays. Make indents with finger; pierce with skewer at 1cm intervals. Cover, stand in warm place about 15 minutes or until risen slightly. Brush focaccias with combined remaining oil and garlic; sprinkle with fine sea salt and seeds. Bake in hot oven 10 minutes, reduce heat to moderate, bake about 15 minutes.

Makes 4.

■ Best made on day of serving.
■ Storage: Airtight container.
■ Freeze: Suitable.
■ Microwave: Not suitable.

BLUE CHEESE AND TOMATO PINWHEELS

2 cups (300g) self-raising flour
30g butter
1 teaspoon cracked black
    peppercorns
1 egg, lightly beaten
2/3 cup (160ml) milk, approximately
1/4 cup (60ml) sun-dried tomato
    tapenade
1/2 teaspoon poppy seeds
1/2 teaspoon sesame seeds

FILLING
1 tablespoon olive oil
1 medium (150g) onion, chopped
2 bacon rashers, chopped
1/4 cup chopped fresh parsley
125g soft blue vein cheese,
    chopped

Sift flour into medium bowl, rub in butter. Stir in pepper, egg and enough milk to mix to a soft, sticky dough. Turn dough onto floured surface, knead until smooth. Roll dough to a 30cm x 35cm rectangle, spread with tapenade, then filling. Roll up from long side, like a Swiss roll; cut into 9 slices.

Place slices, cut side up, in greased 23cm square slab cake pan; sprinkle with combined seeds. Bake in hot oven about 15 minutes. Stand 10 minutes before turning onto wire rack to cool.
Filling: Heat oil in pan, add onion and bacon, cook, stirring, until onion is soft; cool 5 minutes. Stir in parsley and cheese; cool 5 minutes.

Makes 9.

■ Best made just before serving.
■ Freeze: Not suitable.
■ Microwave: Filling suitable.

From left: Blue Cheese and Tomato Pinwheels; Sun-Dried Capsicum and Tomato Focaccias.

FETA AND TOMATO DAMPERS

2 teaspoons olive oil
1 medium (150g) onion, sliced
2 cups (300g) self-raising flour
¾ cup (150g) crumbled feta cheese
1 tablespoon chopped fresh basil
1 tablespoon chopped fresh
　oregano leaves
½ cup (75g) drained, chopped
　sun-dried tomatoes in oil
1 cup (250ml) milk, approximately

Heat oil in pan, add onion, cook, stirring, until onion is soft; cool 5 minutes. Sift flour into large bowl, add onion mixture, two-thirds of the cheese, herbs and tomatoes. Stir in enough milk to mix to a sticky dough, turn onto floured surface, knead until mixture comes together. Divide dough into 6 pieces, shape into rounds. Mark 1cm-deep wedges in dampers, sprinkle with remaining cheese. Place dampers on greased oven trays. Bake in moderately hot oven about 20 minutes.

Makes 6.
■ Best made on day of serving.
■ Storage: Airtight container.
■ Freeze: Not suitable.
■ Microwave: Not suitable.

TOMATO GRISSINI

Grissini can be sprinkled with poppy or sesame seeds, pepper or salt.

1 teaspoon dry yeast
½ cup (125ml) warm water
2 teaspoons honey
2 cups (300g) plain flour
1 teaspoon table salt
2 tablespoons milk
20g butter, melted
¼ cup (40g) grated romano cheese
½ cup (75g) drained, finely chopped
　sun-dried tomatoes in oil
1 tablespoon chopped fresh
　oregano leaves
2 teaspoons chopped fresh thyme

Combine yeast, water and honey in small bowl, whisk until yeast is dissolved. Cover, stand in warm place about 10 minutes or until mixture is frothy. Sift flour and table salt into large bowl, stir in milk, butter, cheese and yeast mixture. Turn dough onto floured surface, knead about 5 minutes or until smooth and elastic. Knead tomatoes and herbs into dough.

Divide dough in half, roll each half to a 15cm x 25cm rectangle. Cut rectangles widthways into 5mm strips, gently roll strips into 17cm sausage shapes. Place grissini about 2cm apart on greased oven trays, brush with a little water, sprinkle with either sesame seeds or poppy seeds, fine sea salt or pepper. Cover with damp cloth, stand in warm place about 5 minutes or until slightly risen. Bake in moderately hot oven about 15 minutes or until lightly browned. Transfer to wire racks to cool.

Makes about 50.
■ Can be made a day ahead.
■ Storage: Airtight container.
■ Freeze: Not suitable.
■ Microwave: Not suitable.

LEFT: From left: Tomato Grissini; Feta and Tomato Dampers.
RIGHT: From left: Tomato Cheese Shortbread; Chilli Tomato Pretzels.

CHILLI TOMATO PRETZELS

1/3 cup (50g) drained sun-dried
    tomatoes in oil
1/2 teaspoon dried crushed chillies
1 teaspoon dry yeast
1/2 teaspoon sugar
1/2 cup (125ml) warm water
1 1/2 cups (225g) plain flour
1/2 teaspoon table salt
2 teaspoons olive oil
1 egg, lightly beaten
1 teaspoon sea salt, approximately

Process tomatoes and chillies until smooth. Combine yeast, sugar and water in small bowl, whisk until yeast is dissolved. Cover, stand in warm place about 10 minutes or until mixture is frothy. Sift flour and table salt into large bowl, stir in oil, tomato mixture and yeast mixture.

Turn dough onto floured surface, knead about 10 minutes or until smooth and elastic. Roll dough to a 15cm x 30cm rectangle, cut widthways into 5mm strips. Gently roll strips into sausage shapes, shape into pretzels. Place pretzels about 2cm apart on greased oven trays, brush with egg; sprinkle with sea salt. Bake in moderate oven about 12 minutes or until firm and lightly browned; cool on trays.

Makes about 60.

- Can be made a day ahead.
- Storage: Airtight container.
- Freeze: Not suitable.
- Microwave: Not suitable.

TOMATO CHEESE SHORTBREAD

2 cups (300g) plain flour
200g butter, chopped
3/4 cup (60g) finely grated fresh
    parmesan cheese
1 tablespoon water, approximately

FILLING
2/3 cup (50g) coarsely grated fresh
    parmesan cheese
1/2 cup (70g) slivered almonds
1/2 cup firmly packed fresh
    basil leaves
1 cup (150g) drained sun-dried
    tomatoes in oil
1/4 cup (60ml) olive oil

Serviette, plate and silver from Made on Earth; round board from The Pacific East India Company

Sift flour into large bowl, rub in butter. Stir in cheese and enough water to make ingredients cling together. Turn dough onto floured surface, knead until smooth. Divide dough in half, roll each half between sheets of baking paper to a 12cm x 35cm rectangle.

Remove top sheets of paper, carefully spread filling over dough. Using bottom sheets of paper as a guide, roll up dough tightly from long side. Gently shape rolls into triangular blocks, wrap in plastic wrap, freeze about 30 minutes or until firm.

Remove plastic wrap. Using a serrated knife, cut shortbread into 1cm slices. Place slices, cut side up, about 2cm apart on lightly greased oven trays. Bake in moderately slow oven about 30 minutes or until lightly browned. Stand 5 minutes before lifting onto wire racks to cool.

Filling: Process cheese, nuts and basil until finely chopped. Add tomatoes, process until combined. Add oil gradually in a thin stream while motor is operating; process until smooth.

Makes about 50.

- Can be made a day ahead.
- Storage: Airtight container.
- Freeze: Not suitable.
- Microwave: Not suitable.

OLIVE SPIRAL LOAF WITH TOMATO BUTTER

2 teaspoons (7g) dry yeast
1 teaspoon sugar
1¼ cups (310ml) warm milk
3½ cups (525g) plain flour
1 teaspoon salt
¼ cup (60ml) olive oil
¼ cup (60ml) tomato paste
½ cup (60g) seeded black olives, finely chopped
½ cup (75g) drained, finely chopped sun-dried tomatoes in oil
2 tablespoons plain flour, extra

TOMATO BUTTER
250g butter, softened
¼ cup (30g) seeded black olives, chopped
1 medium (190g) tomato, peeled, seeded, chopped

Combine yeast, sugar and milk in small bowl, whisk until yeast is dissolved. Cover, stand in warm place about 10 minutes or until mixture is frothy. Sift flour and salt into large bowl, stir in oil, paste and yeast mixture; mix to a firm dough. Turn dough onto floured surface, knead about 10 minutes or until smooth and elastic. Place dough in greased bowl, cover, stand in warm place about 1 hour or until dough has doubled in size.

Knead dough on floured surface until smooth, press into a 23cm x 28cm rectangle. Spread olives and tomatoes over dough, leaving a 2cm border. Roll up dough from long side like a Swiss roll, tuck ends under, place on greased oven tray. Sift extra flour over loaf.

Using scissors, make 6 shallow cuts about 3cm apart across centre. Cover loaf, stand in warm place about 30 minutes or until risen. Cover loosely with foil, bake in moderately hot oven about 1 hour. Serve bread warm with tomato butter.

Tomato Butter: Beat butter in small bowl with electric mixer until light and fluffy, stir in olives and tomato.

◼ Best made on day of serving.
◼ Storage: Airtight container.
◼ Freeze: Suitable.
◼ Microwave: Not suitable.

CARAMELISED ONION AND TOMATO BREAD

3 cups (450g) plain flour
2 teaspoons (7g) dry yeast
2 teaspoons sugar
2 teaspoons salt
2 tablespoons olive oil
1 cup (250ml) warm buttermilk
¼ cup (60ml) water, approximately
2 tablespoons grated fresh parmesan cheese
1 egg, lightly beaten

TOPPING
4 medium (760g) tomatoes
80g butter
2 medium (300g) onions, sliced
1 clove garlic, crushed
¼ cup (55g) sugar

Sift flour into large bowl, stir in yeast, sugar, salt and oil. Stir in buttermilk and enough water to mix to a soft, sticky dough. Turn dough onto floured surface, knead about 10 minutes or until smooth and elastic. Place dough in greased bowl, cover, stand in warm place about 1 hour or until dough has doubled in size.

Knead dough on floured surface until smooth, shape into a 70cm sausage, join ends to make a ring. Place ring on greased oven tray. Cut a 1cm deep slash around centre on top of ring, fill with topping, sprinkle with cheese. Stand, uncovered, in warm place about 30 minutes or until risen; brush dough with egg. Bake in moderate oven about 50 minutes. Cover with foil during baking, if browning too much.

Topping: Peel tomatoes, remove seeds, roughly chop tomatoes. Melt butter in pan, add onions, garlic and tomatoes, cook, stirring, until onions are soft. Add sugar, stir over low heat until sugar is dissolved. Simmer, uncovered, stirring occasionally, about 40 minutes or until mixture is thick and caramelised; cool 10 minutes.

◼ Bread best made on day of serving.
◼ Storage: Airtight container.
◼ Freeze: Not suitable.
◼ Microwave: Not suitable.

From left: Caramelised Onion and Tomato Bread; Olive Spiral Loaf with Tomato Butter.

Wire basket from The Pacific East India Company; plate from Storehouse; serviette from Home & Garden on the Mall

Tray from Made on Earth; terracotta containers from The Pacific East India Company; serviette from Storehouse

PANCETTA TOMATO PLAIT

3 teaspoons (10g) dry yeast
1½ teaspoons sugar
¾ cup (180ml) warm milk
¼ cup (60ml) warm water
2½ cups (375g) plain flour
1 teaspoon table salt
30g butter, melted
¾ cup (110g) drained, chopped
sun-dried tomatoes in oil
8 slices (80g) pancetta
1 teaspoon sea salt

ROCKET PESTO
1 bunch (120g) rocket
¼ cup (20g) grated fresh
parmesan cheese
1 clove garlic, crushed
2 tablespoons olive oil

Combine yeast, sugar, milk and water in small bowl, whisk until yeast is dissolved. Cover, stand in warm place about 10 minutes or until mixture is frothy. Sift flour and table salt into large bowl, stir in butter and yeast mixture. Turn dough onto floured surface, knead about 10 minutes or until smooth and elastic. Place dough in greased bowl, cover, stand in warm place about 1 hour or until doubled in size.

Knead dough on floured surface until smooth, divide into 3 pieces. Roll each piece to a 12cm x 30cm rectangle. Spread each rectangle with rocket pesto, leaving a 1cm border; sprinkle with tomatoes. Roll up from long side, like a Swiss roll. Place rolls on greased oven tray. Plait rolls, join side up, weaving pancetta between strands of plait.

Cover, stand in warm place about 30 minutes or until risen, brush with a little milk; sprinkle with sea salt. Bake in moderately hot oven about 40 minutes or until well browned.

Rocket Pesto: Process rocket, cheese and garlic until smooth. Add oil gradually in a thin stream while motor is operating; process until combined.

- Best made on day of serving.
- Storage: Airtight container.
- Freeze: Suitable.
- Microwave: Not suitable.

ABOVE: Pancetta Tomato Plait.
RIGHT: Roasted Tomato and Fresh Sage Rolls.

ROASTED TOMATO AND FRESH SAGE ROLLS

4 small (240g) egg tomatoes
1 tablespoon fine sea salt
3 teaspoons (10g) dry yeast
1 teaspoon sugar
½ cup (125ml) warm water
½ cup (125ml) warm milk
2½ cups (375g) plain flour
1 teaspoon table salt
1 tablespoon olive oil
¼ cup chopped fresh sage
1 tablespoon milk
¼ cup (30g) grated tasty
   cheddar cheese
¼ cup (20g) coarsely grated fresh
   parmesan cheese

Halve tomatoes lengthways. Place tomatoes, cut side up, on wire rack over baking dish, sprinkle with half the sea salt. Bake, uncovered, in hot oven 40 minutes, cover with foil, bake about 30 minutes or until soft and slightly shrivelled; cool to room temperature.

Combine yeast, sugar, water and milk in small bowl, whisk until yeast is dissolved. Cover, stand in warm place about 10 minutes or until mixture is frothy. Sift flour and table salt into large bowl, stir in oil, sage and yeast mixture.

Turn dough onto floured surface, knead about 10 minutes or until smooth and elastic. Place dough in greased bowl, cover, stand in warm place about 1 hour or until doubled in size.

Knead dough on floured surface until smooth, divide into 8 pieces, shape into balls. Cut a 1cm-deep x 5cm-long cross in each roll, pull cross open to make a place for a tomato half. Brush rolls with milk, place a tomato half on each roll. Sprinkle with combined cheeses and remaining sea salt. Place rolls on lightly greased oven trays, cover, stand in warm place about 30 minutes or until risen. Bake in moderately hot oven about 25 minutes.

Makes 8.

■ Best made on day of serving.
■ Storage: Airtight container.
■ Freeze: Not suitable.
■ Microwave: Not suitable.

Bowl from Home & Garden on the Mall; serviette from Storehouse; wire whisk from The Pacific East India Company

From left: Tomato and Crunchy Seed Damper; Chilli Salami Muffins.

CHILLI SALAMI MUFFINS

2 teaspoons olive oil
1 small (80g) onion, finely chopped
1 teaspoon sambal oelek
1 tablespoon tomato paste
8 slices (40g) hot salami,
    thinly sliced
2 tablespoons drained, chopped
    sun-dried tomatoes in oil
1½ cups (225g) self-raising flour
2/3 cup (100g) plain flour
2 tablespoons chopped
    fresh parsley
½ cup (40g) coarsely grated fresh
    parmesan cheese
2 eggs, lightly beaten
1 cup (250ml) buttermilk
60g butter, melted

TOPPING
8 slices (40g) hot salami,
    thinly sliced
2 teaspoons sesame seeds

Grease 6 hole (3/4 cup/180ml capacity) muffin pan. Heat oil in pan, add onion, cook, stirring, until onion is soft. Add sambal oelek, paste and salami, cook, stirring, 1 minute. Remove from heat, add tomatoes; cool.

Sift flours into large bowl, stir in onion mixture, half the parsley and remaining ingredients. Spoon mixture into prepared pan; sprinkle with topping. Bake in moderately hot oven about 25 minutes or until browned.

Topping: Combine remaining parsley with salami and seeds in small bowl; mix well.

Makes 6.

■ Best made on day of serving.
■ Storage: Airtight container.
■ Freeze: Suitable.
■ Microwave: Not suitable.

TOMATO AND CRUNCHY SEED DAMPER

2½ cups (375g) white
    self-raising flour
½ cup (80g) wholemeal
    self-raising flour
50g butter
2 tablespoons sunflower
    seed kernels
2 tablespoons pumpkin
    seed kernels
2 tablespoons sesame seeds
¼ cup (35g) drained, chopped
    sun-dried tomatoes in oil
2 tablespoons drained, chopped
    sun-dried capsicums in oil
½ cup (125ml) milk
1 cup (250ml) water, approximately

Sift flours into large bowl, rub in butter, stir in all seeds, tomatoes and capsicums. Add milk and enough water to mix to a soft, sticky dough. Turn dough onto floured surface, knead until smooth. Shape dough into a 15cm round, place on greased oven tray. Mark a 1cm-deep cross on round, brush with a little extra milk, sprinkle with a little extra flour and extra sesame seeds, if desired. Bake in moderately hot oven about 30 minutes.

■ Best made just before serving.
■ Freeze: Suitable.
■ Microwave: Not suitable.

HOT AND SPICY CALZONES

2 teaspoons (7g) dry yeast
1 teaspoon sugar
1½ cups (375ml) warm water
4 cups (600g) plain flour
1 teaspoon salt
2 tablespoons chopped fresh
   coriander leaves
2 tablespoons olive oil
150g mozzarella cheese,
   thinly sliced

FILLING
1 tablespoon olive oil
1 large (200g) onion, chopped
3 cloves garlic, crushed
125g button mushrooms, sliced
1 large (350g) red pepper, chopped
1 (180g) chorizo sausage, sliced
80g sliced hot salami, chopped
2 tablespoons drained, chopped
   sun-dried tomatoes in oil
2 tablespoons tomato paste
3 teaspoons sambal oelek
2 tablespoons chopped fresh
   coriander leaves

TOMATO COULIS
2 medium (380g) tomatoes,
   chopped
2 tablespoons tomato paste
¼ cup (60ml) water

Combine yeast, sugar and water in small bowl, whisk until yeast is dissolved. Cover, stand in warm place about 10 minutes or until mixture is frothy. Sift flour and salt into large bowl, add coriander, oil and yeast mixture; mix to a firm dough. Turn dough onto floured surface, knead about 10 minutes or until smooth and elastic. Place dough in greased bowl, cover, stand in warm place about 45 minutes or until doubled in size.

Knead dough on floured surface until smooth. Divide dough into 4 pieces, roll each piece to a 22cm round. Place rounds on greased oven trays. Top each round with quarter of the filling and quarter of the cheese. Fold rounds in half to enclose filling, press edges together. Brush calzones with a little milk. Cut 2 small slits on top of each calzone. Bake in hot oven about 20 minutes or until browned. Serve with tomato coulis.

Filling: Heat oil in pan, add onion and garlic, cook, stirring, until onion is soft. Add mushrooms, pepper, sausage and salami, cook, stirring, until pepper is just soft. Stir in combined remaining ingredients; cool.

Tomato Coulis: Combine all ingredients in small pan, simmer, uncovered, about 5 minutes or until mixture has thickened slightly. Blend or process mixture until smooth.

Makes 4.

■ Filling and tomato coulis can be made a day ahead.
■ Storage: Covered, in refrigerator.
■ Freeze: Not suitable.
■ Microwave: Not suitable.

BELOW: Hot and Spicy Calzones.
RIGHT: Mexican Muffins.

MEXICAN MUFFINS
1/2 x 400g can tomatoes
2 cups (300g) self-raising flour
1/2 cup (85g) cornmeal
3/4 cup (90g) grated smoked cheese
2 small fresh red chillies, chopped
2 tablespoons chopped fresh coriander leaves
130g can creamed corn
1/4 cup (60ml) vegetable oil
1/4 cup (60ml) milk
1 egg, lightly beaten
1 tablespoon cornmeal, extra
1/4 teaspoon ground sweet paprika

TOMATO CORIANDER CREAM
1 medium (190g) tomato
1 cup (250ml) sour cream
2 tablespoons chopped fresh coriander leaves

Grease 6 hole (3/4 cup/180ml capacity) muffin pan. Drain tomatoes well, chop tomatoes. Sift flour into large bowl, stir in cornmeal, cheese, chillies, coriander, corn, tomatoes, oil, milk and egg. Spoon mixture into prepared pan; sprinkle with extra cornmeal and paprika. Bake in moderately hot oven about 25 minutes. Serve with tomato coriander cream.

Tomato Coriander Cream: Quarter tomato, remove seeds, finely chop tomato. Combine tomato with remaining ingredients in small bowl; mix well.

Makes 6.

■ Best made on day of serving.
■ Storage: Muffins, in airtight container. Tomato coriander cream, covered, in refrigerator.
■ Freeze: Muffins suitable.
■ Microwave: Not suitable.

POTATO, TOMATO AND ROSEMARY FOCACCIA

2¹⁄₃ cups (350g) plain flour
¹⁄₂ teaspoon salt
2 teaspoons (7g) dry yeast
**¹⁄₄ cup (20g) grated fresh
    parmesan cheese**
**2 teaspoons finely chopped
    fresh rosemary**
2 tablespoons olive oil
1 cup (250ml) warm water
1 medium (200g) potato
3 medium (570g) tomatoes
8 small sprigs fresh rosemary
1 tablespoon olive oil, extra

Sift flour and salt into large bowl, stir in yeast, cheese, chopped rosemary, oil and water; mix to a firm dough. Turn dough onto floured surface, knead about 10 minutes or until smooth and elastic. Place dough on greased oven tray, press into a 25cm round, cover, stand in warm place about 1 hour or until dough has doubled in size.

Peel potato, cut potato into 2mm slices. Peel tomatoes, cut tomatoes into 1cm slices; remove seeds. Overlap potato and tomato slices on dough, top with rosemary sprigs, drizzle with half the extra oil. Bake in moderately hot oven about 45 minutes; brush with remaining oil. Sprinkle with freshly ground black pepper, if desired.

■ Best made just before serving.
■ Freeze: Not suitable.
■ Microwave: Not suitable.

TOMATO, CUMIN AND BURGHUL BREAD

¹⁄₄ cup (40g) burghul
2 teaspoons (7g) dry yeast
2 teaspoons sugar
1 cup (250ml) warm water
3 cups (450g) plain flour
¹⁄₄ cup (40g) polenta
2 teaspoons salt
¹⁄₄ cup (60ml) olive oil
¹⁄₄ cup (60ml) tomato paste
2 teaspoons ground cumin
1 egg, lightly beaten
2 teaspoons cumin seeds

TOMATO BUTTER
250g butter
**³⁄₄ cup (110g) drained sun-dried
    tomatoes in oil**
1 clove garlic, crushed
**2 tablespoons chopped fresh
    oregano leaves**

Place burghul in small bowl, cover with cold water, stand 15 minutes. Drain burghul, rinse under cold water, drain; blot dry with absorbent paper.

Combine yeast, sugar and water in small bowl, whisk until yeast is dissolved. Cover, stand in warm place about 10 minutes or until mixture is frothy. Sift flour into large bowl, stir in polenta, salt, oil, paste, ground cumin, burghul and yeast mixture. Turn dough onto floured surface, knead about 10 minutes or until smooth and elastic. Place dough in greased bowl, cover, stand in warm place about 1¹⁄₂ hours or until doubled in size.

Knead dough on floured surface until smooth. Divide dough in half, roll each half to a 10cm x 20cm rectangle. Roll up from long side like a Swiss roll, shape gently into ovals. Place loaves seam-side down on greased oven trays, cover, stand in warm place about 20 minutes or until risen. Make 3 slashes on loaves, brush with egg, sprinkle with cumin seeds. Bake in moderately hot oven about 35 minutes.
Tomato Butter: Process all ingredients until well combined.

Makes 2.
■ Best made on day of serving.
■ Storage: Airtight container.
■ Freeze: Suitable.
■ Microwave: Not suitable.

From left: Potato, Tomato and Rosemary Focaccia; Tomato, Cumin and Burghul Bread.

Glass stand and knife from Made on Earth

Drinks

Tomatoes make refreshing drinks, offering the perfect combination of tang and sweetness. These imaginative drinks will both pick you up and cool you down on a hot summer day and are great to serve at parties.

Jug and glasses from Home & Garden on the Mall

DEVIL'S FURY

2 cups (500ml) tomato juice
1 cup (250ml) orange juice
1 cup (250ml) apple juice
1 cup (250ml) gin
1/3 cup (75g) sugar
1/2 teaspoon Tabasco sauce

Combine all ingredients in jug, stir until sugar is dissolved; cover, refrigerate.

Makes about 1.25 litres (5 cups).

■ Best made at least 3 hours ahead.

SPICED TOMATO LIQUEUR

1 medium (180g) orange
4 medium (760g) tomatoes, chopped
3 1/2 cups (770g) sugar
2 cups (500ml) water
1 cinnamon stick
4 cloves
6 black peppercorns, crushed
2cm piece fresh ginger, peeled, sliced
2/3 cup (160ml) vodka

Using a vegetable peeler, peel 6 thin strips of rind from orange. Combine rind, tomatoes, sugar, water, spices and ginger in large pan, stir over heat, without boiling, until sugar is dissolved. Simmer, uncovered, without stirring, about 15 minutes or until liquid is reduced by about one-third. Strain through muslin, discard pulp. Stir in vodka, pour into hot sterilised bottles, seal immediately; refrigerate.

Makes about 1 litre (4 cups).

■ Best made a week ahead.

TOMATO, APPLE AND GINGER PUNCH

1 medium (150g) apple
2 tablespoons grated fresh ginger
125g strawberries, quartered
2 cups (500ml) apple juice
1 1/2 cups (375ml) tomato juice
3 cups (750ml) dry ginger ale

Peel, core and chop apple. Press ginger between 2 teaspoons to extract juice; discard pulp. Combine apple and strawberries in large jug, add ginger juice and remaining juices; mix well. Cover, refrigerate until cold. Just before serving, add cold ginger ale.

Makes about 2 litres (8 cups).

■ Recipe, without ginger ale, can be made a day ahead.

MINTED TOMATO, RHUBARB AND LIME COOLER

4 cups (440g) chopped rhubarb
1/4 cup (55g) sugar
1/4 cup (60ml) water
4 medium (760g) tomatoes, peeled, seeded, chopped
2 1/2 tablespoons lime juice
3 cups ice cubes
2 tablespoons chopped fresh mint

Combine rhubarb, sugar and water in medium pan, simmer, covered, about 10 minutes or until rhubarb is tender; cool. Just before serving, blend or process rhubarb with remaining ingredients until smooth.

Makes about 1.25 litres (5 cups).

■ Best made just before serving.

TOMATO, WATERMELON AND PINEAPPLE SLUSH

1 large (2kg) pineapple, peeled, cored, chopped
700g piece watermelon, peeled, chopped, seeded
4 medium (760g) tomatoes, peeled, seeded, chopped
1 tablespoon icing sugar mixture, approximately

Blend or process pineapple until almost smooth, press through fine sieve; discard pulp. Blend or process watermelon,

tomatoes and 1/2 cup (125ml) of the pineapple liquid until smooth, press through fine sieve; discard pulp.

Combine remaining pineapple liquid with watermelon mixture in large jug; stir in enough sugar to sweeten to taste. Pour into 20cm x 30cm lamington pan, cover, freeze until just firm.

Just before serving, chop fruit mixture; process in batches until smooth and changed in colour.

Makes about 1.25 litres (5 cups).
■ Can be made a day ahead.

PEACHY TOMATO ICED TEA

1 litre (4 cups) boiling water
6 peach-flavoured tea bags
2 cups (500ml) peach nectar
3 large (750g) tomatoes,
**   roughly chopped**
1 tablespoon sugar

Combine water and tea bags in large heatproof jug; mix well, cover, cool to room temperature. Squeeze tea bags to extract as much flavour as possible; discard bags. Blend or process nectar, tomatoes and sugar until smooth, press

firmly through fine sieve; discard pulp. Combine tomato mixture with tea in jug; mix well, cover, refrigerate.

Makes about 1.5 litres (6 cups).
■ Best made on day of serving.

From left: Tomato, Apple and Ginger Punch; Peachy Tomato Iced Tea; Minted Tomato, Rhubarb and Lime Cooler; Tomato, Watermelon and Pineapple Slush; Spiced Tomato Liqueur; Devil's Fury.

Mint

Tarragon

Glossary

Here are some terms, names and alternatives

to help everyone use and understand our recipes perfectly.

Curly parsley

ALLSPICE: pimento.

ALMONDS:

Blanched: kernels with skin removed.

Ground: we used packaged, commercially ground nuts unless otherwise specified.

Slivered: blanched nuts cut lengthways.

BACON RASHERS: bacon slices.

BALMAIN BUG: crustacean; a type of crayfish.

BARBECUE SAUCE: a spicy sauce available from supermarkets.

BEANS:

Black-eyed: black-eyed peas.

Broad (fava): available fresh, frozen and dried.

Cannellini (butter): small white beans.

Green (French): top and tail before use.

Lima, dried baby white: Madagascar beans.

BEEF:

Chuck steak: from the neck area.

Fillet steak (eye-fillet): tenderloin.

Minced: ground beef.

BEETROOT: regular round beet.

BELACAN (also belachan and blachan): dried shrimp paste sold in slabs or flat cakes.

BREADCRUMBS:

Packaged: use fine packaged breadcrumbs.

Stale: use 1- or 2-day-old bread made into crumbs by grating, blending or processing.

BURGHUL (bulghur wheat or bulgar): wheat grains are steamed, dried and crushed; do not confuse with cracked wheat.

BUTTER: use salted or unsalted (also called sweet) butter; 125g is equal to 1 stick butter.

CAPERS: pickled buds of a Mediterranean shrub.

CAYENNE PEPPER: chilli pepper.

CHEESE:

Blue vein: we used a firm blue cheese.

Bocconcini: small balls of mild, delicate cheese packaged in water or whey to keep them white and soft.

Cream: also known as Philly.

Feta: a soft Greek cheese with a sharp, salty taste.

Gruyere: a Swiss cheese with small holes and a nutty, slightly salty flavour.

Haloumi: a firm, cream-coloured sheep's milk cheese; a little like feta in flavour.

Mozzarella: a fresh, semi-soft cheese with a delicate, clean, fresh curd taste; has a low melting point and stringy texture when heated.

Parmesan: sharp-tasting hard cheese.

Ricotta: fresh, unripened, light curd cheese.

Romano: hard cheese; straw-coloured with a grainy texture and sharp, tangy flavour.

Smoked: use a firm smoked cheese.

Soft blue vein: soft, creamy, sweet cheese with delicate blue veining.

Tasty cheddar: mature-tasting, firm-textured cheese.

CHICK PEAS: garbanzos.

CHILLIES: available in many different types and sizes. Use rubber gloves when chopping fresh chillies as they can burn your skin. Discard seeds and membranes to reduce heat.

Dried crushed: available from supermarkets and Asian food stores.

Fresh green poblano: long, dark green chilli with a rich flavour.

Powder: the Asian variety is the hottest, made from ground chillies; it can be used as a substitute for fresh chillies in the proportion of 1/2 teaspoon ground chilli powder to 1 medium chopped fresh chilli.

CHOCOLATE, BITTERSWEET: good-quality eating chocolate with a low sugar content.

CHORIZO: spicy sausage with pork.

COCONUT:

Cream: available in cans and cartons.

Milk: available in cans.

CORNFLOUR: cornstarch.

CORNMEAL: ground corn (maize); similar to polenta but pale yellow and finer. One can be substituted for the other, but results will vary.

COUSCOUS: a fine cereal made from semolina.

CREAM (minimum fat content 35%): fresh pouring cream.

Sour (minimum fat content 35%): a thick commercially cultured soured cream.

CRUSHING SEEDS: seeds and spices can be crushed with a mortar and pestle or by using an attachment to a hand-held processor; or, the side of a heavy, large-bladed kitchen knife or cleaver.

CURRY LEAVES: available fresh or dried; they have a mild curry flavour.

CURRY POWDER: a convenient combination of powdered spices. It consists of chilli, coriander, cumin, fennel, fenugreek and turmeric in varying proportions.

EGGPLANT: aubergine.

ENGLISH SPINACH: a soft-leaved vegetable; young silverbeet can be substituted.

FISH SAUCE: made from liquid derived from salted, fermented anchovies. Has a strong smell and taste; use sparingly. Several varieties are available and the intensity of flavour varies. We used Thai fish sauce.

FLOUR:

White plain: all-purpose flour.

White self-raising: substitute plain (all-purpose) flour and baking powder in the

Fresh curry leaves

Coriander

Balmain bug

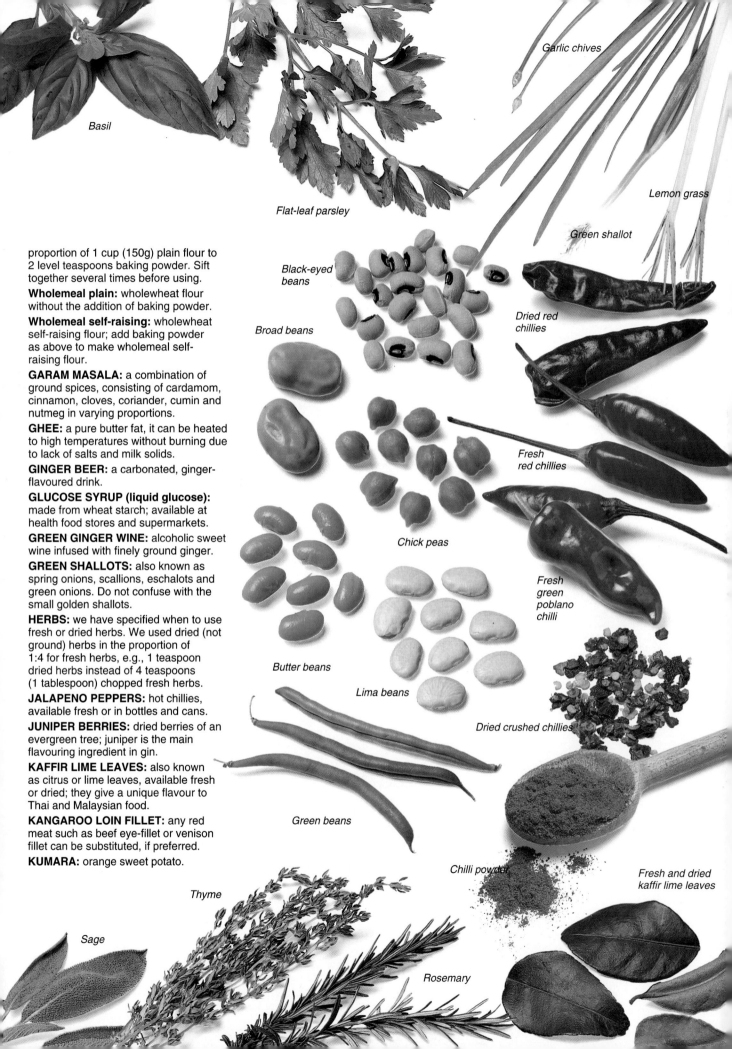

Basil

Flat-leaf parsley

Garlic chives

Lemon grass

Green shallot

Black-eyed beans

Broad beans

Dried red chillies

Fresh red chillies

Chick peas

Fresh green poblano chilli

Butter beans

Lima beans

Dried crushed chillies

Green beans

Chilli powder

Fresh and dried kaffir lime leaves

Sage

Thyme

Rosemary

proportion of 1 cup (150g) plain flour to 2 level teaspoons baking powder. Sift together several times before using.

Wholemeal plain: wholewheat flour without the addition of baking powder.

Wholemeal self-raising: wholewheat self-raising flour; add baking powder as above to make wholemeal self-raising flour.

GARAM MASALA: a combination of ground spices, consisting of cardamom, cinnamon, cloves, coriander, cumin and nutmeg in varying proportions.

GHEE: a pure butter fat, it can be heated to high temperatures without burning due to lack of salts and milk solids.

GINGER BEER: a carbonated, ginger-flavoured drink.

GLUCOSE SYRUP (liquid glucose): made from wheat starch; available at health food stores and supermarkets.

GREEN GINGER WINE: alcoholic sweet wine infused with finely ground ginger.

GREEN SHALLOTS: also known as spring onions, scallions, eschalots and green onions. Do not confuse with the small golden shallots.

HERBS: we have specified when to use fresh or dried herbs. We used dried (not ground) herbs in the proportion of 1:4 for fresh herbs, e.g., 1 teaspoon dried herbs instead of 4 teaspoons (1 tablespoon) chopped fresh herbs.

JALAPENO PEPPERS: hot chillies, available fresh or in bottles and cans.

JUNIPER BERRIES: dried berries of an evergreen tree; juniper is the main flavouring ingredient in gin.

KAFFIR LIME LEAVES: also known as citrus or lime leaves, available fresh or dried; they give a unique flavour to Thai and Malaysian food.

KANGAROO LOIN FILLET: any red meat such as beef eye-fillet or venison fillet can be substituted, if preferred.

KUMARA: orange sweet potato.

Juniper berries

Rocket

Arborio rice

Brown rice

Wild rice

Basmati rice

LAMB

Cutlet: small, tender rib chop.

Fillet: tenderloin; the smaller piece of meat from a row of loin chops or cutlets.

Leg: from the hindquarter.

Minced: ground lamb.

Rack: row of cutlets.

Shank: forequarter leg.

LAMINGTON PAN: 20cm x 30cm cake pan, 3cm deep.

LEBANESE CUCUMBER: thin-skinned variety also known as European or burpless cucumber.

LEEK: a member of the onion family, resembles the green shallot but is much larger.

LEMON GRASS: available fresh from Asian food stores.

MADEIRA: wine fortified with brandy.

MILK: we used full-cream homogenised milk unless otherwise specified.

Buttermilk: made by adding a culture to a low-fat milk to give a slightly acidic flavour; a low-fat milk can be substituted.

MIXED SPICE: a blend of ground spices usually cinnamon, allspice and nutmeg.

MUSHROOMS:

Button: small, unopened mushrooms with a delicate flavour.

Flat: large, soft, flat mushrooms with a rich earthy flavour.

Oyster: pale grey-white mushrooms; shaped like a fan.

Shiitake: used mainly in Chinese and Japanese cooking.

Swiss brown: light to dark brown mushrooms with full-bodied flavour. Button or cup mushrooms can be substituted for Swiss brown mushrooms.

MUSTARD:

Dijon: a hot French mustard.

Dry: available in powder form.

French: plain mild mustard.

Hot English: extremely hot mustard, made from mustard seeds, wheat flour and turmeric.

Mild English: a milder mustard.

Seeded: a French-style coarse mustard.

Seeds: can be black or yellow.

NOODLES, THICK FRESH RICE: flat noodles; available from Asian food stores and supermarkets.

OIL:

Chilli: oil infused with chillies.

Extra virgin and virgin: the highest quality olive oils, obtained from the first pressings of the olives.

Light: mild tasting, light in flavour, colour and aroma, but not lower in kilojoules.

Macadamia: oil extracted from macadamia nuts.

Olive: a blend of refined and virgin olive oils, especially good for everyday cooking.

Peanut: made from ground peanuts, mostly used in Asian cooking; a lighter salad type of oil can be substituted.

Sesame: an oil made from roasted, crushed white sesame seeds; is used for flavouring, not frying.

Vegetable: polyunsaturated vegetable oil.

PANCETTA: cured pork belly; bacon can be substituted.

PAPRIKA: ground dried peppers, available sweet or hot.

PEPPERS: capsicum or bell peppers; remove seeds and membranes.

PINE NUTS: small, cream-coloured soft kernels.

POLENTA: usually made from ground corn (maize); similar to cornmeal but coarser and darker in colour. One can be substituted for the other but results will be slightly different.

PRAWNS: shrimp.

PROSCIUTTO: uncooked, unsmoked, cured ham; ready to eat when bought.

PUMPKIN SEEDS: pepitas.

RHUBARB: a vegetable with pinkish stalks that are generally cooked and eaten as a fruit.

RICE:

Arborio: large round-grained rice especially suitable for risotto.

Basmati: a white, fragrant long-grained rice.

Brown: natural whole grain.

Wild: from North America, but not a member of the rice family.

RIND: zest.

ROCKET: also arugula, rugula and rucola; a green salad leaf.

SAFFRON: available in strands or ground form. The quality varies greatly.

Finger eggplant

Eggplant

Silverbeet

English spinach

SAMBAL OELEK: also ulek or olek: a salty paste made from ground chillies.

SESAME SEEDS: there are 2 types, black and white; we used white in this book.

SILVERBEET (Swiss chard): Remove coarse white stems; cook green leafy parts as required by recipes.

SOY SAUCE: sometimes spelled soya; made from fermented soya beans.

SPATCHCOCK: small chicken weighing around 500g.

SPICY ITALIAN SAUSAGES: fresh, spicy beef sausages; butchers make their own variations.

SUGAR: we used coarse granulated table sugar, also known as crystal sugar, unless otherwise specified.

Brown: a soft, fine-granulated sugar containing molasses which gives characteristic colour.

Caster: also known as superfine; is fine-granulated table sugar.

Icing sugar mixture: also known as confectioners' sugar or powdered sugar, with the addition of cornflour.

Pure icing: also known as confectioners' sugar or powdered sugar.

SULTANAS: golden raisins.

SUN-DRIED CAPSICUMS: dried capsicums bottled in oil; available at specialty stores and some supermarkets.

TABASCO SAUCE: made with vinegar, hot red peppers and salt.

TAHINI: made from crushed sesame seeds.

TOASTING: to toast seeds, nuts, coconut, etc., spread evenly onto oven tray, toast in moderate oven a few minutes or stir in heavy-based pan over heat until golden brown.

TOMATO:

Canned: whole peeled tomatoes in natural juices.

Green: we used under-ripe tomatoes, not the green variety tomato.

Juice: commercially made by squeezing tomatoes through a machine that removes the seeds and skins. It is undiluted pure juice.

Paste: a concentrated thick paste made from tomato puree. It is called tomato puree in some countries. It is used for flavouring soups, stews, sauces and casseroles, etc.

Puree: canned, pureed tomatoes (not tomato paste). Also known as Passata in some countries. Use fresh, peeled, pureed tomatoes as a substitute, if preferred.

Sauce: tomato ketchup.

Sun-dried: dried tomatoes, available bottled in oil or dry-packed.

Sun-dried tomato tapenade: available from specialty stores.

VINEGAR:

Balsamic: originated in the province of Modena, Italy. Regional wine is specially processed then aged in antique wooden casks to give a pungent flavour.

Brown: made from fermented malt and beech shavings.

Cider: vinegar made from fermented apples.

Red wine: based on red wine.

Rice wine: mild and slightly sweet, made from fermented rice.

White: made from spirit of cane sugar.

White wine: based on white wine.

YEAST: allow 2 teaspoons (7g) dry yeast to each 15g compressed yeast if substituting one for the other.

ZUCCHINI: courgette.

Flat mushrooms

Shiitake mushrooms

Button mushrooms

Oyster mushrooms

Swiss brown mushrooms

HOW TO PEEL AND SEED TOMATOES

1. Remove stem end from tomatoes with the point of a sharp knife.

2. Place tomatoes in large bowl, cover with boiling water, stand about 30 seconds or until skins begin to lift. Transfer tomatoes to large bowl of cold water, stand about 30 seconds or until cool enough to handle. Skins should peel away easily.

3. Cut tomatoes in half, scrape seeds out carefully with a teaspoon.

4. Alternatively, squeeze tomatoes gently to remove seeds.

Tips on Preserving

Many of the preserves recipes make large quantities, so they are ideal gifts.

■ Fruits and vegetables used in preserving must be clean, unblemished and well washed.

■ Use good-quality vinegars containing at least 4% acetic acid; cheap vinegars do not contain enough acetic acid to act as a preservative.

■ Preserves containing oil often turn cloudy in the refrigerator; they will clear on standing at room temperature.

■ We have used minimum salt in our recipes. Taste the preserve before bottling, add salt to suit your taste.

Cooking Equipment

When making preserves, use large wide-topped aluminium, stainless steel or enamel saucepans or boilers; do not use copper or unsealed cast iron pans; the acid in the preserve will damage the metal and colour and flavour ingredients. Do not leave preserve mixtures standing in aluminium pans for more than about an hour.

Jars and Bottles: Sterilising, Sealing and Storage

■ Jars and bottles must be glass, without chips or cracks, and should be thoroughly washed, then sterilised. As a general rule, hot preserves go into hot sterilised jars, cold preserves go into cold sterilised jars.

■ Keep jars covered with clean tea-towel to keep dust-free while preparing preserves. Jars and bottles must be dry. Make sure your hands and tea-towels are clean. Unclean jars can cause deterioration in all preserves.

STERILISING

Method 1: Put clean jars and lids in dishwasher, put through rinse cycle at hottest temperature; do not use detergent.

Method 2: Place clean jars lying down in pan, cover completely with cold water, cover pan, bring to boil, then boil, covered, for 20 minutes. Carefully remove jars from water (use tongs and thick rubber gloves). Drain jars well, stand right way up on clean wooden board. The heat will evaporate any remaining water in the jars.

Method 3: Stand clean jars right way up and not touching on clean wooden board in cold oven; turn oven temperature to very slow, leave for 30 minutes. Remove jars from oven.

SEALING

■ As soon as hot or cold preserves are poured into hot or cold jars or bottles, they must be correctly sealed to prevent deterioration.

■ Metal lids are not suitable; the acid content of the preserve will corrode the lids and the contents will become contaminated. Special lined and treated or lacquered lids, available with home preserving outfits, are suitable to use.

■ Plastic screw-top lids give a good seal (plastic snap-on lids are not airtight enough). Plastic lids must be well washed, rinsed and dried, or put through the dishwasher.

■ Some older preserving outfits have glass lids; these can be sterilised by either of the above methods. Do not use aluminium foil, cellophane or paper covers for preserves; foil will be corroded by the acid in the preserves, paper and cellophane are not airtight enough for long-term keeping.

■ Paraffin wax (available from chemists) makes an excellent seal. Melt slowly over low heat, pour a thin layer, about 2mm, just enough to cover surface, leave until almost set, then pour another thin layer on top of first layer. Insert small pieces of string into wax just before it sets to make it easier to remove wax. It is important not to over-heat wax or it will shrink on cooling, giving an imperfect seal. Wipe sealed jars clean, label and date.

STORAGE

Recipes specify whether to store preserves, etc., in a cool, airy, dark, dry place (light can cause deterioration), or in the refrigerator. If you live in a hot or humid climate, the refrigerator is always the safest method of storage. Refrigerate preserves, covered, after opening. There are some recipes in the preserves section which are suitable to freeze. They are marked with the symbol **F**. They must be frozen in suitable clean containers (not glass), leaving about 2cm at the top to allow for expansion, then sealed with a clean clip-on or screw-on lid.

Microwave Cooking

We have not tested these recipes in a microwave oven. However, chutneys, pickles and sauces, etc., can be cooked in small quantities in the microwave oven, but, as evaporation is often necessary, we prefer the conventional way. Relishes are usually fine to microwave; the colour retention is excellent.

Making Jam

■ To test if jam has jelled:
Dip a wooden spoon into the mixture, hold spoon above mixture and tilt the bowl of the spoon towards you; as mixture cooks and thickens, the drops will fall more heavily from the spoon. When it is ready, 2 or 3 drops will roll down the edge of the spoon and join together in a heavy mass.

When this happens, remove jam from heat to stop further cooking, allow bubbles to subside, then drop a teaspoon of mixture onto a chilled saucer (the freezer is best), return saucer to freezer until jam is at room temperature, not frozen.

■ Jam containing pieces of fruit surrounded by jelly should have formed a skin which will wrinkle when pushed with the finger.

■ Jam which is pulpy in texture should be of a spreadable consistency.

■ When jam is at jelling stage, skim surface, if necessary. If jam contains pieces of fruit, let it stand for 5 to 10 minutes (depending on the size and type of fruit used) before bottling. This allows the mixture to cool slightly and the fruit to disperse more evenly.

■ Jams made from pulpy fruit such as tomatoes, strawberries, etc., should be bottled immediately; they have reached the desired consistency.

Note: Jams will reach jelling point at 105°C to 106°C (220°F to 222°F). A candy thermometer can be used for testing.

■ Be careful when handling hot jam. Pour jam into hot sterilised jars right to the top of the jar, jam will shrink on cooling.

■ Seal jars immediately. Label jam and store in a cool, dark, airy place, or, if you live in a hot or humid climate, store in refrigerator. If jam has been cooked and sealed correctly, it will keep for at least 12 months. Once opened, store in refrigerator.

■ If jam has not set after testing, return to heat, retest after 5 minutes. Times are only a guide; the variations in fruit and size of pans used must be considered.

■ The quicker jam reaches the correct stage, the better it will be in flavour and clarity. Always use a pan proportionate to the amount of jam you are making. As a guide, roughly measure the depth of the mixture, using a wooden spoon, **after** the sugar has been added; it should not be more than 5cm deep at this stage.

Index

MAKE YOUR OWN STOCK

If you prefer to make your own stock, these recipes can be made up to 4 days ahead and stored, covered, in the refrigerator. Be sure to remove any fat from the surface after the cooled stock has been refrigerated overnight. If the stock is to be kept longer, it is best to freeze it in smaller quantities. Stock is also available in cans or tetra packs. Stock cubes or powder can be used. As a guide, 1 teaspoon of stock powder or 1 small crumbled stock cube mixed with 1 cup (250ml) water will give a fairly strong stock. Be aware of the salt and fat content of cubes and powders and prepared stocks.

BEEF STOCK

2kg meaty beef bones
2 medium (300g) onions
2 sticks celery, chopped
2 medium (250g) carrots, chopped
3 bay leaves
2 teaspoons black peppercorns
5 litres (20 cups) water
3 litres (12 cups) water, extra

Place bones and unpeeled chopped onions in baking dish. Bake in hot oven about 1 hour or until bones and onions are well browned. Transfer bones and onions to large pan, add celery, carrots, bay leaves, peppercorns and water, simmer, uncovered, 3 hours. Add extra water, simmer, uncovered, further 1 hour; strain.

CHICKEN STOCK

2kg chicken bones
2 medium (300g) onions, chopped
2 sticks celery, chopped
2 medium (250g) carrots, chopped
3 bay leaves
2 teaspoons black peppercorns
5 litres (20 cups) water

Combine all ingredients in large pan, simmer, uncovered, 2 hours; strain.

FISH STOCK

1.5kg fish bones
3 litres (12 cups) water
1 medium (150g) onion, chopped
2 sticks celery, chopped
2 bay leaves
1 teaspoon black peppercorns

Combine all ingredients in large pan, simmer, uncovered, 20 minutes; strain.

VEGETABLE STOCK

2 large (360g) carrots, chopped
2 large (360g) parsnips, chopped
4 medium (600g) onions, chopped
12 sticks celery, chopped
4 bay leaves
2 teaspoons black peppercorns
6 litres (24 cups) water

Combine all ingredients in large pan, simmer, uncovered, 1½ hours; strain.

**All stock recipes make about
2.5 litres (10 cups).**

QUICK CONVERSION GUIDE

Wherever you live in the world you can use our recipes with the help of our easy-to-follow conversions for all your cooking needs. These conversions are approximate only. The difference between the exact and approximate conversions of liquid and dry measures amounts to only a teaspoon or two, and will not make any difference to your cooking results.

MEASURING EQUIPMENT

The difference between measuring cups internationally is minimal within 2 or 3 teaspoons' difference. (For the record, 1 Australian metric measuring cup will hold approximately 250ml.) The most accurate way of measuring dry ingredients is to weigh them. When measuring liquids use a clear glass or plastic jug with metric markings.

If you would like the measuring cups and spoons as used in our Test Kitchen, turn to page 128 for details and order coupon. In this book we use metric measuring cups and spoons approved by Standards Australia.

● a graduated set of four cups for measuring dry ingredients; the sizes are marked on the cups.
● a graduated set of four spoons for measuring dry and liquid ingredients; the amounts are marked on the spoons.
● 1 TEASPOON: 5ml.
● 1 TABLESPOON: 20ml.

NOTE: NZ, CANADA, USA AND UK ALL USE 15ml TABLESPOONS.
ALL CUP AND SPOON MEASUREMENTS ARE LEVEL.

DRY MEASURES

METRIC	IMPERIAL
15g	½oz
30g	1oz
60g	2oz
90g	3oz
125g	4oz (¼lb)
155g	5oz
185g	6oz
220g	7oz
250g	8oz (½lb)
280g	9oz
315g	10oz
345g	11oz
375g	12oz (¾lb)
410g	13oz
440g	14oz
470g	15oz
500g	16oz (1lb)
750g	24oz (1½lb)
1kg	32oz (2lb)

LIQUID MEASURES

METRIC	IMPERIAL
30ml	1 fluid oz
60ml	2 fluid oz
100ml	3 fluid oz
125ml	4 fluid oz
150ml	5 fluid oz (¼ pint/1 gill)
190ml	6 fluid oz
250ml	8 fluid oz
300ml	10 fluid oz (½ pint)
500ml	16 fluid oz
600ml	20 fluid oz (1 pint)
1000ml (1 litre)	1¾ pints

WE USE LARGE EGGS WITH AN AVERAGE WEIGHT OF 60g

HELPFUL MEASURES

METRIC	IMPERIAL
3mm	⅛in
6mm	¼in
1cm	½in
2cm	¾in
2.5cm	1in
5cm	2in
6cm	2½in
8cm	3in
10cm	4in
13cm	5in
15cm	6in
18cm	7in
20cm	8in
23cm	9in
25cm	10in
28cm	11in
30cm	12in (1ft)

HOW TO MEASURE

When using the graduated metric measuring cups, it is important to shake the dry ingredients loosely into the required cup. Do not tap the cup on the bench, or pack the ingredients into the cup unless otherwise directed. Level top of cup with knife. When using graduated metric measuring spoons, level top of spoon with knife. When measuring liquids in the jug, place jug on flat surface, check for accuracy at eye level.

OVEN TEMPERATURES

These oven temperatures are only a guide; we've given you the lower degree of heat. Always check the manufacturer's manual.

	C° (Celsius)	F° (Fahrenheit)	Gas Mark
Very slow	120	250	1
Slow	150	300	2
Moderately slow	160	325	3
Moderate	180 – 190	350 – 375	4
Moderately hot	200 – 210	400 – 425	5
Hot	220 – 230	450 – 475	6
Very hot	240 – 250	500 – 525	7

TWO GREAT OFFERS FROM THE AWW HOME LIBRARY

Here's the perfect way to keep your Home Library books in order, clean and within easy reach. More than a dozen books fit into this smart silver grey vinyl folder. PRICE: Australia $11.95; elsewhere $21.95; prices include postage and handling. To order your holder, see the details below.

All recipes in the AWW Home Library are created using Australia's unique system of metric cups and spoons. While it is relatively easy for overseas readers to make any minor conversions required, it is easier still to own this durable set of Australian cups and spoons (photographed). PRICE : Australia: $5.95; New Zealand: $A8.00; elsewhere: $A9.95; prices include postage & handling
This offer is available in all countries.

TO ORDER YOUR METRIC MEASURING SET OR BOOK HOLDER:
PHONE: Have your credit card details ready. Sydney: (02) 260 0035; **elsewhere in Australia:** 008 252 515 (free call, Mon-Fri, 9am-5pm) or FAX your order to (02) 267 4363 or MAIL your order by photocopying or cutting out and completing the coupon below.
PAYMENT: **Australian residents:** We accept the credit cards listed, money orders and cheques. **Overseas residents:** We accept the credit cards listed, drafts in $A drawn on an Australian bank, also English, New Zealand and U.S. cheques in the currency of the country of issue.
Credit card charges are at the exchange rate current at the time of payment.

Please photocopy and complete coupon and fax or send to:
AWW Home Library Reader Offer, ACP Direct, PO Box 7036, Sydney 2001.

❏ Metric Measuring Set ❏ Holder

Please indicate number(s) required.

Mr/Mrs/Ms _____

Address_____

_____

Postcode _____ Country_____

Ph: ( ) _____Bus. Hour: _____

I enclose my cheque/money order for $_____ payable to ACP Direct

OR: please charge my:
❏ Bankcard ❏ Visa ❏ MasterCard ❏ Diners Club ❏ Amex

❏❏❏❏❏❏❏❏❏❏❏❏❏❏❏❏❏❏ Exp. Date ___/__

Cardholder's signature _____

(Please allow up to 30 days for delivery within Australia. Allow up to 6 weeks for overseas deliveries.)

Both offers expire 30/6/97.   AWSF97